Off the Field and On

Triumphs and Trials of Gaelic Games

BRENDAN FULLAM is a native of Ardagh, County Limerick,
and a retired bank manager, who served in that capacity
in Killorglin, County Kerry, the Crescent in Wexford, and
New Ross. In his younger years his banking career took him to
Killorglin, Kilrush, Clifden, Ballyshannon, Wexford and Tralee,
and in each of these towns he played with the local hurling
team. Gaelic Games are his passion, and his vision in meeting
and interviewing the legends of hurling resulted in three unique
and invaluable records of the game and its players — *Giants of
the Ash*, *Hurling Giants* and *Legends of the Ash*. He is also author
of *The Wolfhound Guide to Hurling* (1999).

To my grandchildren
Caroline, Gráinne, Emmet, Patrick, Daniel,
Tom, Niamh, Aodán and Eoghan

May they cherish and enjoy our national games

Off the Field and On

Triumphs and Trials of Gaelic Games

Brendan Fullam

WOLFHOUND PRESS
Celebrating 25 Years

Published in 1999 by
Wolfhound Press Ltd
68 Mountjoy Square
Dublin 1, Ireland
Tel: (353-1) 874 0354
Fax: (353-1) 872 0207

British Library Cataloguing in Publication Data
A catalogue record for this book is available from the British Library.

ISBN 0-86327-760-8

10 9 8 7 6 5 4 3 2 1

Cover Photographs: Courtesy of Inpho Photography
Cover Design: Azure
Typesetting: Wolfhound Press
Printed in the Republic of Ireland by Colour Books, Dublin.

Contents

FOREWORD

Despite the fact that the GAA is Ireland's largest sporting organisation, there is a great deal of vital and valuable information concerning it not available to the public. Brendan Fullam's *Off the Field and On* is a treasury of information and insight.

Following on his other popular and very readable books, this latest work by Brendan Fullam will be welcomed by all lovers of Gaelic Sports, and the history of those sports.

A clear, energetic, well-informed writer, Brendan Fullam's *Off the Field and On* is a publication that will delight GAA followers.

It will provide the fodder for many a lively conversation. And it will shed new and interesting light on these glorious decades.

Brendan Kennelly
Professor of English
University of Dublin

PREFACE

In my early schooldays very little in the way of printed matter on hurling was available to us young people, or even to our parents. The only daily newspaper on sale in our village was the *Irish Independent*, and its reports on Gaelic games were scant and uninspiring. What we learned about hurling was confined to a great extent to the local scene. The matches between teams drawn from the locality were the main focus of attention — the results were discussed and were often the subject of heated arguments. They might even gain a brief mention on the local paper. Around the firesides at evening time the older people recalled the games of the past, praising the skills of the outstanding players who had gained awards with the county team, and they became our boyhood heroes, although we had never seen them playing. The stories were embellished with snippets of local ballads and songs that have remained a loving memory.

Our Gaelic games' horizons were vastly extended in the following decade as a result of significant advances in the communications media. The *Irish Press* was launched in September 1931 carrying full pages of bright accounts of hurling and football games written by expert reporters, illustrated by banner headlines and head-and-shoulders photographs of individual players. This was a godsend to us young people and we became busy with scissors, cutting out, and pasting into scrapbooks, our favourites and storing them away as prized possessions. Other daily newspapers had to accept and follow the new trend in reporting in order to attract their readers. The players were no longer merely names but now their faces were familiar to us and we recognised them as individuals.

A new dimension in sports communication was added when radio began broadcasting the games over the air. Groups gathered eagerly around the available radio sets enchanted by the word-pictures woven by Mícheál O'Hehir in describing every puck and kick of the ball in the ebb and flow of a game. Listeners felt as if they were present at the game, sharing in its excitements and tensions through the unique power of the broadcaster's voice.

The influence of broadcasts was seen clearly in the remarkable increase in public support for GAA games, swelling the attendances especially at the major games. They also had a part in creating an atmosphere of support for publications dealing with affairs of the Association. *Carbery's Annual* featuring rural activities and the chief Gaelic Games of each year in an attractive personal style, enjoyed a successful run of almost thirty years. Tommy Quaid's periodical *Gaelic Sport* has maintained its steady readership over the past forty years. These successful ventures inspired more initiatives, and when television exposed the games live, more viewers were attracted to them, impressed by the skill and speed of the play, and this in turn brought an increasing demand for more information on the teams and the personalities associated with them. A crop of new publications dealing with the history of the Association appeared on the shelves in the bookstores and the sales showed that there was a ready market for them.

Gradually, county GAA histories began to appear and the example was taken up by individual clubs that were proud to display their part in the growth and development of the success story of the GAA. Eagerly sought were the reminiscences of the great players of the past, recalling the exciting moments in their careers. Bright colourful weekly and monthly GAA magazines, with a wealth of photographs and articles, are taking a more prominent place in town and village stores, and offer a wide choice to the reader. County Year Books have now become an annual feature brought out to capture the Christmas market.

Naturally, I am very pleased (though maybe a little envious) when I see the wide range of reading material that is there for my grandchildren today compared to the meagre lot that we could find in my schooldays. I am thinking especially of the splendid volumes brought out in the past few years by Brendan Fullam. In his youth, Brendan was powerfully attracted to hurling and played with many teams in different places, as he was transferred in his work from town to town. He continued his intense interest in the game all through his life, fascinated by its variety of skill, its speed, its excitement and its power to attract. Attending games and studying teams and players, he amassed a fund of knowledge and experience that could not be contained within his mind, but called for an outlet for publication. Out of his huge fund of memories and his deep researches, he compiled three attractive volumes on hurlers and hurling published by Wolfhound Press in this decade: *Giants of the Ash*, *Hurling Giants* and *Legends of the Ash*, all highly successful publications. They would constitute a massive output from one writer in such a short space of time. But not resting, in this, his fifth book, Brendan has taken a wide sweep with his pen to recall to us over twenty-five key incidents in the life of the GAA; from its birth to the present day, from the first All-Ireland finals to the controversy regarding last year's championship.

Many will have heard of the Cooney case of 1938 but how many are aware of the facts of the case? And fewer still know the extent of the controversy it gave rise to. How many hurling finals produced no goals by the winners, and could you imagine a final when no points were scored by the winners? These are some of the fascinating matters recounted in this new volume.

Brendan looks on all his writing as a debt paid for the wonderful enjoyment he got out of playing hurling in his youth, and the inexpressible pleasure he got from attending many great hurling occasions down the years.

I am honoured to be allowed to be associated in a small way with the launching of this book. My thanks to you, Brendan, for inviting me to write a Foreword to it. I am proud to do so.

Séamus Ó Riain
President of the GAA 1967-1970

No more I'll join the cross-roads dance,
Or mow the blooming clover,
Or share the joys with the girls and boys
When the harvest day is over;
No more upon the hurling field
Will Sunday evenings find me,
But far away from all that's gay
And the spot I've left behind me.

'Sliabh Ruadh'

The present meets the past,
The future, too, is there.

The Origin of a National Legend

It began a revolt against degradation, leading to submission;
A recall to the past so that its glories might again animate us;
A tocsin for the present so that the future should find us united
and strong and fit to be freemen.

Celt

Michael Cusack, Maurice Davin and Dr Thomas William
Croke were the triumvirate that formed the pillars on which the
Gaelic Athletic Association was built. From these foundations
the GAA not only grew, but prospered and developed into the
greatest amateur athletic organisation the world has ever known.
Conor Cruise O'Brien described it as:

> *More than the Gaelic League, more than Arthur Griffith's Sinn Féin,
> more even than the Transport and General Workers' Union and, of
> course, far more than the movement which created the Abbey Theatre;
> more than any of these the Gaelic Athletic movement aroused the
> interest of large numbers of ordinary people throughout Ireland. One of
> the most successful and original mass-movements of its day, its
> importance has, perhaps, not even yet been fully recognised.*

In *The Shaping of Modern Ireland*, Professor David Greene wrote
of the GAA:

> *It was the first modern example of a great democratic movement, with
> the attendant apparatus of committees and boards, under completely
> Irish auspices.*

The first meeting to establish the GAA took place at Thurles
on Saturday, 1 November 1884, in the Billiard Room of Miss
Hayes's Commercial Hotel. Those present, as recorded in *The
Story of the GAA* by T.F. O'Sullivan, were:

Maurice Davin, Carrick-on-Suir
Michael Cusack, Dublin
John Wyse Power, Naas, Editor of the Leinster Leader
John McKay, Cork, a member of the Reporting Staff of the
Cork Examiner

P.J. O'Ryan, Callan, a young solicitor practising at Callan and Thurles

J.K. Bracken, Templemore, a contractor who erected a number of 1798 Memorials throughout the country

St George McCarthy, Templemore, a young athlete who took no part in the promotion of the Association after the first meeting (he subsequently became a District Inspector of Constabulary)

The object of the meeting was:

... to take steps for the formation of a Gaelic Association for the preservation and cultivation of our national pastimes and for providing national amusements for the Irish people during their leisure hours.

Cusack had been alarmed by the cultural decline in Ireland, the aimlessness of youth, and the extent to which apathy had gripped the people. He felt it was vital that Irish people should take the management of their own games and athletics into their own hands.

Following the Thurles meeting, no time was lost in inviting prominent Irishmen to become patrons of the Gaelic Athletic Association.

On 18 December 1884, the most Reverend T.W. Croke, Archbishop of Cashel and Emly, responded to the invitation in a famous letter that subsequently became described as the charter of the GAA.

Charles S. Parnell acknowledged his invitation of 11 December in his reply dated 17 December from Irish Parliament Offices, London. He accepted ' ... with appreciation the position of Patron of the Association which has been offered to me'. On 21 December, Michael Davitt, writing from the Imperial Hotel, Dublin, accepted ' ... with great pleasure the position of Patron which has been assigned me by the GAA'.

The Patronage of these three individuals gave the movement a tremendous boost. Other prominent names were soon added to the list, John O'Leary, the noted Fenian, William O'Brien, M.P. and Douglas Hyde, President of the Gaelic League (founded in 1893).

The foregoing list of names represents a great cross-section of support from leading Irish individuals. Their patronage enabled the ideals and objectives of the GAA to radiate out among the ordinary people. It also enabled Cusack to declare that the 'association swept the country like a prairie fire'. A renaissance had begun.

The new movement uplifted the spirit of a downtrodden people and made them proud of their heritage; it presented them with an all-important badge of identity.

However, all was not smooth nor plain sailing during the organisation's early days. There were many obstacles and many stormy moments, opposition from without and dissension from within. However, the GAA survived and grew from strength to strength. Today, it has become a magnificent national institution that has served the nation very well.

On 31 July 1893 Douglas Hyde (son of a Church of Ireland Rector, born in Sligo in 1863 and raised at French Park, County Roscommon); Eoin MacNeill (born in 1867, at Glenarm, County Antrim, and the first to suggest the creation of a movement to bring the language to the people); Fr Eugene O'Growney (author and Professor of Irish at Maynooth College), together with eight others, met and founded Conradh na Gaeilge. Its philosophy was based on the concept of an Irish Ireland and its objectives were the revival of Irish and all things Irish; it was to become a great inspiration to the people of Ireland.

Non-religious and non-political, Conradh na Gaeilge attracted members from all walks of life — ranging (on the political spectrum) from the staunchest nationalist to the most steadfast Orangeman. It became a firm ally of the GAA and both organisations worked hand in hand in the promotion of national ideals.

Thus, towards the end of the nineteenth century, three key movements were established that played a major part in shaping the future social and cultural life of this country. The Land League which secured, through 'The Fall of Feudalism', the future of land ownership; the Gaelic Athletic Association which nurtured our games and Conradh na Gaeilge which sought to preserve our beautiful language. *Ní tír gan teanga.* (Thomas Davis, the young Irelander, once wrote — 'A nation without a language is only half a nation'.)

Michael Cusack.

Michael Cusack was born in Carron, in the Barony of Burren, County Clare on 20 September 1847. He was a native Irish speaker, nationalist, visionary, athlete, sportsman and idealist. As he grew up he observed the grip the ruling classes of the day had on all affairs including sports and pastimes. He also noted the extent to which the ordinary people were excluded from such activities. Cusack resolved to remedy matters. He believed the solution lay in the revival of our culture, pastimes, games, music and song, all of which were, at that time, at a very low ebb.

Michael Cusack was a product of the times in which he lived and he proved to be just the man to lead the cultural crusade. He was a man of vigour, stamina and patriotic resolve. It is said that his special love was hurling.

Having qualified as a National teacher, he began his career at Lough Cutra National School near Gort, in County Galway and remained there until October 1871. Prior to setting up his own private Academy in Dublin, he taught English and Mathematics at St Colman's College, Newry, until 1874. He was also a Professor at Blackrock College and spent some time at St John's College, Kilkenny, before moving from there to Clongowes Wood.

The following description of Michael Cusack is given in *The Story of the GAA* by T.F. O'Sullivan:

Here is a vivid pen-picture of the Founder of the GAA written by a Dublin gentleman (Mr Joseph Maguire BL) who was personally acquainted with him:

'In the closing years of the last century a striking figure would sometimes be met with in the streets of the Irish metropolis, and one that seldom failed to attract the attention of the passer-by, whether citizen or stranger. It was a man of middle height, with handsome features, dark eyes, black hair and a beard, and with a scholarly roundness of the shoulders, which combined with their great breadth, detracted from the apparent height of their owner, making him look shorter in stature than he really was. He usually wore a broad rimmed soft hat, and in defiance of the prevailing fashion, always wore knee breeches instead of trousers. The habitual expression of his face was serious, and his stride, as he walked, self-reliant, even combative — an effect which was heightened by

the large blackthorn he invariably carried. Those familiar with the main thoroughfare of Dublin at the period referred to, may easily recognise in this brief description the figure of the late Michael Cusack, a man of intensely Irish character and sympathies, a scholar, an athlete, and an Irish-Irelander of the most pronounced type ... Cusack who had a magnificent constitution from his early boyhood took a keen interest in athletics. As a member of the Leinster Football Association he played a good deal of rugby and also competed in weight-throwing competitions at athletic meetings.

Cusack was a Nationalist of a robust, healthy type, and all the sympathies of his early manhood went out to the unselfish Irishmen identified with the '67 Movement. Long before the establishment of the Gaelic League, he was an earnest worker in the cause of the language revival. He was a trenchant writer, and a ready and fluent public speaker — qualities which he utilised to the full in the momentous campaign in which he was entering at this stage of his career — the establishment of the Gaelic Athletic Association.'

Although removed from his position as Secretary in 1886 he remained active in, and supportive of, the GAA for the rest of his life.

Michael Cusack, who liked to be called Citizen Cusack, died on 27 November 1906, a little over two months after his fifty-ninth birthday.

Is fíor go mbíonn an beagán ann i gcónaí a dheineann morán ar son a dtíre agus ina measc siud tá Mícheál Cíosóg ón gCarn, gaiscíoch na Bóirne, fear a bhí Gaelach go smior. Ar dheis Dé go raibh a anam uasal.

Sean Mac Conmara (Br)

Maurice Davin

Maurice Davin was born in Carrick-on-Suir on 29 June 1842. As he grew to manhood he developed into a magnificent physical specimen and became an outstanding all-round athlete who played a variety of sports.

He excelled as an oarsman, and in the field of athletics he was outstanding at weight-throwing and jumping. He defeated all comers at national and international athletic contests. In the first ever international competition between Ireland and England in 1876, he broke the world record at hammer-throwing. He held the world hammer-throw record from 1875 to 1880 and also held the world record for the 56lb weight competitions. He was also an accomplished cricket player and even did a bit of boxing.

The common denominator of interest in sports brought Davin and Cusack together and they jointly signed the circular convening the Thurles meeting of 1884. The following is the text of that circular:

> *Dear Sir — You are earnestly requested to attend a meeting which will be held at Thurles on 1st Nov. to take steps for the formation of a Gaelic Association for the preservation and cultivation of our national pastimes and for providing national amusements for the Irish people during their leisure hours. The movement which it is proposed to inaugurate has been approved of by Mr. Michael Davitt, Mr. Justin McCarthy, M.P.; Mr. William O'Brien, M.P.: Mr. T. Harrington, M.P.; and other eminent men who are interested in the social elevation of the race. The place of the meeting will be determined on at The Commercial Hotel, Thurles, at 2 o'clock on the day of the meeting.*

> *Maurice Davin, Carrick-on-Suir,*
> *Michael Cusack, Dublin, Hon. Sec. pro tem.*
> *N.B. The favour of a reply is requested. – Michael Cusack*

Maurice Davin was elected as the GAA's first President, on the 1 November 1884. He drafted the rules for the new Association which were submitted and adopted at a meeting on 17 January 1885. He was also one of the main contributors to the revised constitution, which was adopted at the second annual convention in 1886. It aimed at providing greater control of the Association's affairs and the elimination of abuses. Article 14 stated 'that no new rule should be introduced, nor any of the foregoing altered, except at a meeting of the General Committee called for that purpose'. The Executive Committee held a meeting on 27 February 1887, from which Davin was unavoidably absent, during which some new rules were adopted by those members who were present.

Davin found such action most disturbing. He could not understand how those entrusted with maintaining the constitution would break its rules in this way. He resigned his position as President when they failed to revoke the decision that had been taken at the executive meeting in February.

Davin was a constitutionalist and a moderate — 'a man of giant strength and ability ... equally high qualities of mind and head'. He was a firm leader, with a calm disposition. Through the mediation of Dr Croke, talks with Maurice Davin and Michael Davitt, took place at the Archbishop's Palace in Thurles on 22 November 1887. As a result of these discussions, the Association was reconstructed in 1888, and Maurice Davin resumed his position as President.

He preferred accord to discord as the following appeal for unity shows:

> One of the objects of the founders of the Gaelic Athletic Association was to put down factions and make you good friends with one another. Do not allow your association to be split up in parties by anyone. There is no reason why it should. Union amongst Irishmen was never more wanted than at the present.

The character and nature of the man is further illustrated in a letter written on 20 February 1885 to Mr J.G. Beatty, Secretary of the Irish Athletic Clubs. At that time suspicion existed in some athletic quarters towards the new body, the GAA, and it led to considerable friction.

Maurice Davin wrote:

> Dear Sir — I have asked Mr. Cusack, Hon. Secretary of the Gaelic Association, to attend your meeting on 21st inst., if he thinks well of doing so. I do this, as I think matters may be brought forward which it would be well to have explained on the spot. If this were done it would prevent bad feeling between parties. There should be no ill-will between athletes. Men may hold different opinions on many subjects, and yet be friends.
>
> Yours truly, Maurice Davin

The chairman said there could not be a nicer letter than that.

Maurice Davin was 65 years old when William Fletcher visited him at his home in Deerpark, Carrick-on-Suir, and wrote the following account of him in the New York Daily News:

> As the old champion came down the walk he moved erect with an easy stride. He was so broad that his well-set shoulders and massive chest entirely filled the walk. He stood 6'1", weighed 225 lbs and measured 48" round the chest. His hair and beard were snow white; his eyes were bright and sparkling and there was a rosy glow of health on his cheeks. His heart burns fiercely with love for Ireland and glows warm for any athlete who is devoted to the sports at which he excelled. He lets you know his home is yours when you visit him.

He resigned the Presidency at the Annual Convention of 1888 which was held in Thurles on 23 January 1889. He left the meeting following controversy over the 1888 finances of the Association, for which he was not at all responsible. However, his deep interest in the affairs of the GAA continued even though he never returned to the Association's councils.

He died on 26 January 1927 at his home in Deerpark, Carrick-on-Suir.

Dr Thomas W. Croke

From the outset the Archbishop of Cashel, Dr Thomas W. Croke, was tremendously supportive of the objectives and ideals of the GAA. On 16 September 1885, he sent a cheque for £10 to the Association. The following is an excerpt from his covering letter:

> Ever since I have become connected, as a Patron, with your association, I have been thinking of offering a small prize to be competed for under your rules, in any way and wherever you please. For, as a leader is one who leads, so a Patron is one who patronises, and patronage is surely of little worth if it brings no substantial profit to the person or society to which it is extended. Perhaps, indeed, as you are about to hold, I hear, a championship meeting at Tramore early next month, the time and place would be deemed opportune for the furtherance of my purpose.
>
> Anyhow I enclose a cheque for £10 to be disposed of as your Executive may think fit, for the benefit of the Gaelic Athletic Association, and am, dear Mr Cusack, your very faithful servant,
>
> T.W. Croke.

Replying to addresses from branches of the Association, at Charleville on Sunday, 24 July 1887, the Archbishop said:

> As one of the Patrons of the Association, I have every reason to congratulate myself and the country at large on the rapid progress made by the Association and on the corresponding impulse given to those fine national sports of which our fathers were so justly proud, but which a spurious taste for foreign athletic importations had long extinguished amongst us.'

The following is an excerpt from the Preface to the *Rules and Constitution of the Association* written by Michael Davitt (Rule Book 1888) under the pen name 'Mulla':

The name of the Archbishop of Cashel was connected with it from the outset. His patronage was a tower of strength to the organisation from its infancy. His pen was frequently employed in its support. When, later, the Gaelic ship was on the point of sailing into troubled waters, and the enemies of our name and race rejoiced over the fact, it was his wise advice and his disinterested mediation that steered the association into a haven of security and peace, where it now moves free and fearless with well-trimmed sails, its colours mast high, and plain for all good folk to see.

The GAA paid special tribute to Dr Croke on the occasion of his Episcopal Silver Jubilee on 18 July 1895. He, in turn, presented two silver cups to the Association in 1896 for football and hurling competitions. (In the 1896 competitions Clare beat Wexford at hurling 6:16 to 0:2 on 27 June 1897 while Dublin beat Tipperary at football 0:4 to 0:3 on 13 June 1897.)

In the 1897 hurling competition, Limerick beat Kilkenny 3:8 to 1:4 at Thurles on 9 July 1899. (In the early days of the GAA, finals were not always played in the same year as that in which a championship had started. This occurred for various reasons ranging from general disputes, political unrest, and the social upheaval of the War of Independence and the Civil War.) Dr Croke attended the game and imparted his blessing to the kneeling players after being presented to them by Frank B. Dinneen, Secretary of the Association. (The football competition was won by Wexford when they defeated Cork 1:11 to 0:2 on 28 May 1899.)

Thomas F. O'Sullivan recounted Dr Croke's death in 1902 as follows:

Gaels throughout the length and breadth of Ireland and in foreign lands learned of the death of the Most Rev. Dr. Croke, who passed away on the night of 22nd July, with feelings of the most sincere sorrow. His Grace's famous letter of 18th Dec. 1884 accepting the patronage of the association was one of the greatest factors in developing the infant organisation. Up to the hour of his death the great prelate took a keen interest in the GAA and he watched its steady growth with pride and pleasure. A few words regarding his career may not be out of place here.

Thomas W. Croke was born near the town of Mallow in May 1824. His father was a Catholic and his mother a Protestant. He was only 14 years of age when he entered the Irish College in Paris to prepare for the Sacred Ministry. He left the College in 1844. He then spent a year at the

College of Menin, Belgium, as Professor of English and Mathematics. He resided for three years in the Irish College in Rome, where he took out his D.D. degree. It is stated that the gold and silver medals he won in this College were sent to the jeweller, and the proceeds forwarded to Ireland for the relief of the poor during the terrible famine period. In 1846 he was raised to the dignity of priesthood. On returning to Ireland he began his missionary career in his native parish of Cloyne. Earnest, holy, zealous, and patriotic, he was beloved by those amongst whom he ministered. He was full of animal spirits, and fond of a good joke, a good story, or a good song. He stood over 6 feet, and was a fine specimen of vigorous manhood.

Fr. Croke was appointed Principal of the new Seminary of St. Colman's Fermoy. He was afterwards given Pastoral charge of Doneraile. His fame as a preacher, organiser, and man of talent reached the Vatican, and in 1866 he was raised to the Episcopate as Bishop of Auckland, where for four years he performed magnificent work in clearing off a heavy debt on the Cathedral and perfecting the Catholic organisation throughout the diocese. Owing to his prodigious labours, he was compelled to return to his native land to recruit his health, and while in Ireland he was appointed Archbishop of Cashel in the Summer of 1870 in his forty-sixth year. Dr. Croke's work in Cormac's See is largely the religious and political history of the diocese for over 30 years, and is closely interwoven with the progress of the national movement during that period.

As a youth he was deeply impressed by the principles of the Young Irelanders, and in his more mature manhood, he worked earnestly for the re-establishment of our native Parliament. In 1883, by a generous subscription and an eloquent letter he gave a hearty send-off to the movement started for the purpose of presenting Parnell with a National Testimonial. Owing to his action, and as a result of English influence at the Vatican, he was summoned to Rome, where he pleaded the cause of Ireland with vigour and eloquence before the Sovereign Pontiff. A note was issued from the Vatican, but the National Testimonial was not appreciably affected, and Parnell was presented with £40,000, as an oppressed Nation's tribute to his great work for Ireland. The subsequent history of the Archbishop, so far as it affected the GAA, has been dealt with in these articles, and it is unnecessary to recapitulate it at this stage, except to state that from the moment he became Patron of the Association he lost no opportunity of spreading the Organisation, defending its aims and objects, composing its disputes, presenting it with Cups for competition and identifying himself with it in every possible way.

It was not strange, therefore, that the Gaels of Ireland should feel a peculiar sense of loss when the Crozier fell from the lifeless grasp of its distinguished Patron and Champion; and that resolutions expressive of heartfelt sorrow at his demise, should be passed by the Governing Body of the Association; by the All-Ireland Convention, and County Committees and Clubs throughout the country; and that Gaels were prominent in the cortege which conveyed the aged Prelate to his last resting-place in the town which was the cradle of their Organisation.

Michael Cusack (seated centre with white shirt) and the Metropolitan Hurling Club

Most Rev. Dr Croke, Archbishop of Cashel

Maurice Davin

THE METAMORPHOSIS OF THE CELT

Though still quite young at the time (the writer was born in August, 1872), I well remember the great change that came over the country, and the vivid and lasting impression it made on me. Until then everything was lonely and stagnant in the land, and the young men in their idle hours loitered in dull fashion by the street and fence corners. In a few months how different things became!

The country was soon humming with interest and activity, the ambitions of the young men were aroused, every parish had its newly formed hurling or football team, prepared to do or die for the honour of the little village.

Anon, the war of championships was on! We followed armies of Gaels many miles along the country roads to the field of combat, where as many as eight or ten teams, gaily clad in their coloured jerseys, struggled for supremacy before our dazzled and delighted eyes! How we cheered our beloved heroes on to victory, and what pride we felt in looking on the stalwart and athletic forms! To play on the 'first team' was, indeed, the greatest honour a youth could hope for, and many of us looked forward to that day with swelling hearts!

Reverend James B. Dollard
('Sliav-na-Mon')
in the *Gaelic Athletic Annual for 1907–8*

Father Dollard was an ardent Gael who spent many years in America. His love of homeland and its games was immense and he wrote many poems.

This one, titled 'Our Matchless Hurling Men', reflects his feelings.

See on the green and springy sward
The banded hurlers stand
(Glory and fame their sole reward),
With swift camán in hand!
Ho, knaves and foemen stand aside,
No carpet knights are they!
God save our matchless hurling men,
Our Irish Gaels, hurrah!

THE FIRST FINALS — 1887 CHAMPIONSHIPS

Although the GAA was officially founded in 1884, the All-Ireland hurling and football championships did not begin until 1887. In that first year, the competition operated on an open-draw basis.

Both of the championships were open to all affiliated clubs of the GAA. Only counties which had committees established at the time were eligible to participate and these committees were the forerunners of the county boards.

The following draws were made for both hurling and football in 1887:

Wicklow *v* Clare	Tuesday 19 July in Athlone
Wexford *v* Galway	Sunday 24 July in Dublin
Dublin *v* Tipperary	Saturday 30 July in Mountrath
Cork *v* Kilkenny	Sunday 24 July in Dungarvan
Waterford *v* Louth	Thursday 21 July in Dublin
Limerick *v* Meath	Monday 25 July in Maryboro

Hurling

Wicklow made their exit from the championship following their refusal to travel to Athlone to play Clare — they had considered it an unreasonable journey to make.

Dublin suffered a similar fate when their request to postpone their game with Tipperary was turned down. The request stemmed from the fact that some of their players were on holidays at the time.

Louth and Waterford didn't field hurling teams at all. Meanwhile, Cork were kept out of the hurling championship altogether as a result of a dispute within the county between the finalists, St Finbarr's and Nationals.

At the time there were two county boards in Limerick. So two teams (both claiming to represent the county), Castleconnell and Murroe, travelled to Dublin to play Tullaroan, at Elm Park.

The Central Council suggested that the two teams play each other to decide who would play Tullaroan. The suggestion was turned down and Tullaroan moved on to the next round.

In the end, only five of the counties actually participated in the first year of the championship. Tipperary were drawn against Clare and the match was fixed to be played at Limerick. However, as Clare did not travel, the match was re-fixed for Nenagh where Tipperary (Thurles) defeated Clare (Smith O'Briens) by 1:7 to 0:2, in the encounter.

Tipperary's next game was against Kilkenny in the semi-final. Both teams lined-out at Clonmel but as a result of an infringement of the rules, the match was declared cancelled. It was re-fixed for the following Thursday to be played in Urlingford. Kilkenny objected to five of the Borris players but despite having to find replacements, Tipperary won well — 4:7 to nil.

In a somewhat tempestuous encounter, Galway (Meelick) beat Wexford (Castlebridge) 2:8 to 1 goal, at Elm Park, in Dublin. This victory paved the way for a Tipperary (Thurles) *v* Galway (Meelick) final.

The final took place in Birr on Easter Sunday, 1 April 1888, and trains brought supporters and followers from the surrounding counties. According to folklore, the Tipperary team arrived late to discover that Galway had been awarded the title. It seems that following a brief discussion, Galway sportingly agreed to put their title on the line — the rest is history.

The game was refereed by Patrick White, a native of Toomevara, working in Birr. During his lifetime he became deeply involved with the association in County Offaly.

The teams lined out with 21 players aside. In accordance with the rules of the time, no number of points equalled a goal. A forfeit point was awarded when a player sent the sliotar wide at his own goal-line; the equivalent of a 'seventy' in today's game.

On the morning of the match, there was a dispute in the Tipperary camp over the question of expenses. Consequently, their captain, Denis Maher, and six others — D. Maher, Jack Maher, Con Callanan, Pat Ryan, Mattie Maher and Ned Maher — didn't travel. Jim Stapleton took over the captaincy in the absence of Denis Maher.

Galway were led by their non-playing captain, James Lynam. At half-time, Tipperary were in front, leading by 0:1 to nil. In the second half of the match Tommy Healy, following a pass from Jim Stapleton, wrote his name into hurling folklore by scoring the only goal of the game and the first ever in an All-Ireland final.

In *The Story of the GAA*, T.F. O'Sullivan recalls the match as follows:

> *The game was very vigorously contested from start to finish. A Thurles player was accidentally struck with a hurley on the nose, and had to leave the ground. No substitute was appointed, but shortly afterwards the teams were equal in number when a Meelick man was put off the ground for tripping another player. This player, who took up his position on the sideline, could not refrain from hitting the ball occasionally when it came in his direction, or when his side was particularly hard-pressed. He eventually had to be remonstrated with by the referee, who threatened to award the match to Tipperary if he did not cease taking part in the game.*

The final scoreline read, Tipperary 1 goal: 1 point: 1 forfeit point, to Galway's nil.

Forfeit points were abolished at the Congress of 1888, in Thurles, and were replaced with a forty-yard free. When the forfeit points system was in use, five forfeit points had equalled one point.

The weather was perfect on the day of the final and ground conditions were ideal. Given the scoreline, one can only speculate as to what type of game was played in that very first All-Ireland final. The absence of points suggests that there were very few frees during the match. Alternatively, the low total of points may have been because they were unattractive as no number of them equalled a goal; indeed it may well have been a combination of both of these factors.

The winning Tipperary team as recorded by T.F. O'Sullivan comprised:

*Jim Stapleton (Captain), Matty Maher, Andy Maher, Tom Burke,
Ned Murphy, Tom Stapleton, Jeremiah O'Dwyer, Mick Carroll,
Tom Carroll, Tom Maher, John Leamy, Pat Lambe,
Martin MacNamara, Jack Mockler, Jeremiah Ryan, Dan Ryan,
Jim Dwyer, Ned Bowe, Tommy Healy, Paddy Leahy, Jack Dunne.*

Football

To the modern GAA enthusiast, it may seem strange to relate that Kerry didn't participate in the first All-Ireland football championship. However, the other five Munster counties did, together with the Leinster counties of Kilkenny, Louth, Meath and Wexford.

The following campaigns trace the paths travelled by Limerick (Commercials) — a team consisting of drapers' assistants and shop assistants — and Louth (Dundalk Young Irelands), to the final showdown.

Limerick's first-round match was against Meath (Dowdstown) at Elm Park, Dublin. In what was described as a scientific contest, Limerick won with the score 3:2 to 0:2. Despite his lack of height, Malachi O'Brien of Limerick emerged as the most outstanding man of the 42 players on the day. So captivated was Lord French — he resided at Elm Park — by Malachi's performance that he invited him to dinner after the game.

Limerick's next encounter was against Kilkenny (Kilmacow) who had already beaten Cork (Lees) by 0:4 to nil at Clonturk

The Louth Team
Back Row: *V. Wynne, S. Keating, T. McGuinness, N.Trainor, M.Ward, P. Curtis, T. Murphy, J. King, N. McAllister, J. Maguire, S. Quigley–Morgan, J. Keating, T. Caraher.* **Second Row:** *M. Dobbs, J. Campbell, C. McAllister, M. Carroll, J. Dowdall, H. Fagan, J. McCrave.* **Front Row:** *M. Warren, T. Stewart, J. Connor, E. Goodman, T. O'Rourke.*
Courtesy Cathal MacAllastair

Park, Dublin. The battle between Limerick and Kilkenny was a closely contested game, which was played in stormy conditions and ended in a draw at 1:10 each. The replay took place at Bansha in ideal weather, and Limerick, taking the victory, advanced to the semi-final.

Next they met Tipperary (Templemore) who had knocked out Clare (Newmarket-on-Fergus) with a score of 1:8 to 0:3. Limerick lost this match but, following an objection, a replay was ordered and this time they dominated over Tipperary and made it to the final.

Louth's first game was against Waterford (Ballyduff Lower). It took place at Elm Park on 21 July 1887 and 800 Louth supporters travelled to cheer on their team. At half-time, Waterford led by 0:3 to 0:1. They reinforced this lead early in the second half by adding a fourth point. However, this was to be their last score of the game. After that, Louth dominated with the McAllister brothers, Charlie and Ned, very much to the fore. Charlie scored 1 goal and 1 point in the second half and his goal was a turning point in the game. (Charlie and Ned were very active in the Gaelic League and were co-founders of the Northern Brigade of the IRB.) Midfield supremacy saw Louth finally run up a winning score of 1:8 to 0:4.

The game was refereed by Willie Halpin of Newmarket-on-Fergus. At some stage in the game a little dust-up arose between two opposing players. The referee despatched them to the sideline for two minutes to cool off — a discretion that might well benefit the modern game. The encounter between Louth and Waterford was the first game ever to be played under GAA rules.

Louth's next outing was against Wexford (Castlebridge) on 28 August at Golden Bridge. The team, on reaching Dublin by train, travelled to a hotel in d'Olier Street where they togged out. They then proceeded to the pitch by tram. The attendance was about 5,000 spectators and the game was refereed by J.K. Bracken of Templemore. Louth, playing with the wind in the first half, used the elements to full advantage and led at the interval by 0:7 to nil. The situation was reversed in the second half when Louth failed to register any score and were hard pressed to withstand non-stop pressure from Wexford.

However, they kept the Wexford tally down to five points and emerged as the winners on the score 0:7 to 0:5. Thus Louth had qualified to meet Limerick in the final.

The final was played at the grounds of the Benburb Club at Donnybrook (Clonskeagh) on Sunday 29 April 1888. The Limerick team, described as a powerful side of great dash and courage, travelled to Dublin the previous evening and on Sunday made the journey to the pitch by horse tram.

Louth wore black and green jerseys. Charlie and Ned McAllister were absent from the team because of a family bereavement and their places were taken by Arthur O'Hagan and Tom Lavery. The game was described as fast, clever, scientific and sporting. Louth were ahead 0:3 to 0:1 at half-time but at full time the score read Limerick 1:4; Louth 0:3. So it was that Limerick entered the history books as the first All-Ireland senior football champions. Gate receipts were £300 on the day.

After the game, the Louth captain, Michael John Carroll, made an objection on the grounds that William J. Spain was playing for Limerick illegally. It was alleged that Spain had played club football with Kickhams in Dublin. The objection failed.

A report on the game in *The Freeman* said the final was

...a splendid exhibition of skill, science, speed and stamina; it was a model in every respect, the feeling between the combatants being of the friendliest nature. It was a game won fair and square and without fluke or fortune by the Commercials ... The hand-play, punting and general knackiness of the Dundalk men, of whom Louth may well be proud, could hardly be excelled, but they were unable to withstand the fast, determined charging of the boys from Garryowen ... Mr John Cullinane refereed with great judgement and tact and scrupulous exactness.

John Cullinane, a native of Bansha, County Tipperary, was later to become an MP.

Upon his return to Limerick, Malachi O'Brien was celebrated as a hero. He was a mighty kicker of the ball, acclaimed by many as the outstanding footballer of those early days.

It is interesting to note that Commercials, who represented Limerick in the final, had lost two games on their path to glory. In the Limerick final itself, they had lost to St Michael's and, following an objection, were awarded a replay. They won the replay in a game that saw St Michael's forced to drop five of their original players because they had played rugby. Limerick's defeat at the hands of Tipperary has already been referred to.

In due course many of the Limerick team emigrated to 'far foreign fields'. Before his emigration to America, William J. Spain, a native of Nenagh, became the first dual All-Ireland medal holder after winning the 1889 hurling title with Dublin. In this match, played on 3 November 1889, Dublin (Kickhams) had beaten Clare (Tulla) 5:1 to 1:6. Spain was credited with three of those Dublin goals.

Limerick (Commercials) repeated their All-Ireland success in 1896. Sadly, after that, Limerick football, as a championship force, went into decline and surfaced again only on very rare occasions.

However, Louth did remain a powerful force but their footballing abilities were not reflected in the titles that they won. They captured Leinster crowns in 1909, 1910 and 1912, and the All-Ireland title in 1910 and 1912 — a walkover over Kerry and a win over Antrim, respectively. It was in 1912 that

Limerick Commercials, All-Ireland Champions 1887
Back Row: F. Fitzgibbon, E. Nichols, E. Casey, T. McMahon, P. Keating.
Middle Row: D.H. Liddy, P.S. Reeves, J. Mulqueen, M. Slattery, P. Kelly, T. Kennedy, J. Hyland, R. Normyle, D. Corbett (captain), W. Gunning, W. Cleary, R. Breen, P. Treacy. Front Row: T. McNamara, P.J. Corbett, M. O'Brien, T. Keating. J. Kennedy.

Louth first wore the now familiar red jersey with the white trim.

Further provincial successes followed for Louth in 1943, 1948, 1950, 1953 and 1957. They won the coveted Sam Maguire Cup for the first time in 1957 with a famous victory over Cork. Since then Louth have lived in hope.

Readers will find it hard to believe that Tipperary (Thurles) and Limerick (Commercials) did not get their All-Ireland medals until over a quarter of a century after the finals were played.

The football finalists lined-out as follows:

Limerick

Pat Tracey, (non-playing Captain), Denis Corbett, (goal),
Timothy Fitzgibbon, William Gunning, Richard Breen, John Hyland,
Thomas McNamara, William J. Spain, Patrick J. Corbett,
Michael Slattery, Jeremiah R. Kennedy. Michael Casey,
James Mulqueen, Malachi O'Brien, Patrick Kelly, Timothy Kennedy,
Philip Keating, Willie Cleary, Robert Normoyle, Patrick Reeves,
Thomas Keating, T. McMahon

Louth

Michael John Carroll (Captain), Edward Goodman, John Dowdall,
Henry Fagan, Pat Clarke, Jack Connor, Pat McGuinness,
John Maguire, Arthur O'Hagan, James Campbell, Pat Mangan,
Peter Jackson, Tom Murphy, Edward Murphy, William Wheatly,
Pat McGinn, Edward Feeley, Tom O'Rourke, Tom Lavery,
John McCrane, Jim Keating, Sam Keating (substitute)

In this first year of the All-Ireland championship competitions, controversy had surrounded the rule that defined what constituted a parish. This in turn had led to a good deal of friction. However, the matter was resolved at a meeting of the Executive at Limerick on 11 April 1887. At the meeting, the Executive defined a parish as a district presided over by a parish priest.

A GREAT FOOTBALL FINAL

A Kildare/Kerry Classic

The Great Final of 1903 — home final — which was actually played in 1905, was the sixteenth final since the championships first began in 1887. Without a doubt, it was the most memorable of them all and put Gaelic football firmly on the sporting map by attracting many admirers from outside Gaelic circles.

The contenders were Kerry and Kildare who were meeting for the first time in an All-Ireland final. For Kerry, it was their second All-Ireland final, while Kildare were making their first appearance in this event. Each team fielded seventeen players. But it was no easy contest and it took three meetings before the issue was finally decided. Both teams underwent a most thorough training schedule and this was believed to be the first such step since the championships began.

Kerry had won through in Munster, beating both Clare and Cork to secure their place in the final. To followers of Gaelic games nowadays Kilkenny are associated with hurling only. However, it may come as a surprise to learn that it took three games in the Leinster final before Kildare eventually overcame the Kilkenny team. A disputed Kildare point led to the second replay, and on this occasion Kildare left no doubt about their superiority, winning by 9 points to 1 point.

The Great Final itself was played in Tipperary town on 23 July 1905, with Patrick McGrath as referee. As the game drew to a close, the ball hit a spectator and rebounded back into play, following which Kerry scored a goal. Kildare disputed the score and then the spectators encroached on the pitch. The game was abandoned with the score standing at 1:4 to 1:3 in Kerry's favour. Both teams subsequently agreed to a replay in Cork on 27 August following a directive from Central Council.

Here is how the replay, which was watched by 12,000 people, was described in an article in The *Irish Independent*, *GAA*

Golden Jubilee Number, Easter 1934. The author's name is not given but the style has a definite ring of 'Carbery' about it.

> *So a bright August Sunday in 1905 found record contingents and nation-wide enthusiasm which outshone all GAA fixtures before that date. I had come by push bike from Duhallow, and vividly recall the bright, picturesque contingents. From every town, village, island and hamlet in Kerry high-spirited Kerrymen travelled. Glanmire terminus teemed with Kingdom men of all ages sporting the green and gold badges carrying the clarion call, 'Up Kerry', in bold letters. It became a historic slogan, side by side with the euphonious native war cry, 'Ciaraidhe Abu!'. Wonderful crowds, these; they came in glorious holiday spirit and swept Cork City off its feet.*
>
> *The Kildare and Leinster men were more subdued, but their trains were well filled, and their neat all-white favours were much in evidence, mingling in good-humoured streams with the green and gold streamers of the south-western Gaeltacht. The teams were:*

Kerry

T. O'Gorman (Capt.), J. O'Gorman, D. Curran,
M. McCarthy, C. Healy, J. Buckley, J.J. Fitzgerald, C. Duggan,
A. Stack (Tralee), R. Fitzgerald, P. Dillon (goal), D. Kissane,
D. McCarthy, W. Lynch, J. Myers (Killarney), R. Kirwan,
D. Breen (Castleisland)

Kildare

J. Fitzgerald (goal), J. Murray, J. Gorman, M. Donnelly,
E. Kennedy, M. Fitzgerald, R. Murray, J. Scott, Joyce Conlon
(Roseberry), L. Cribbin, J. Rafferty, W. Merriman, W. Bracken,
W. Losty, M. Kennedy, J. Dunne, J. Wright (Clane)

Kerry v Kildare — at Cork 1903

Cork's Lower Park Grounds were the mecca of endless streams of out-side cars and pedestrians who blackened the long Marino avenue beside the Lee river. Twelve thousand spectators were present when Mr M.F. Crowe (a constructive young Limerick City man who made his name as a referee in Dublin) threw in the ball. Kildare won the toss and opened brilliantly. The perfect fielding and long, accurate kicking of Cribbin, Merriman, and Rafferty in defence surprised spectators, whilst the artistic footwork of Losty, Conlon, Bracken, and Scott in front was a revelation to those who thought Gaelic football a game of strength and force alone.

Kerry were not to be outdone in skill, however. The O'Gorman pair were nimble wingers with grand hands. Stack was a tireless ranger and director of operations. McCarthy, Kirwan and Myers kicked that new yellow ball half a field's length, and in front of all was the tall, rangy scoring brain with craft and art — Dick Fitzgerald — the peerless goal getter and deadly drop-kicker, who revolutionised football attack.

Kerry had an early point. Kildare balanced. Kerry got number two from long range. The ball flew from end to end. Tackling was fierce but honest. Kildare forwards seemed to have a string tied to the ball. Fitzgerald opened the way for Kerry's third, but the men from the Curragh, playing delightful football, balanced with three smart points. Near the half way Kerry were aggressive. Their confident handling and perfect placing set the score 5 to 3 in their favour at half-time.

The ball had burst, and a new one equally lively was requisitioned. Kerry used the wind from Blackrock to good purpose. From Fitzgerald's drive Buckley added Kerry's sixth minor when he charged Donnelly's clearance amidst great excitement. Fitzgerald's brilliancy helped Lynch to score Kerry's seventh point, and the game looked as good as over.

Kildare never relaxed. Larry Cribbin's defence was masterful. J. Fitzgerald held his goal safe. Close to the end Kildare's grand forwards got away to get the score at 4 to 7. Conlon and Losty were still dangerous. Then, four minutes from the end, the All-White men, from a sweeping ball by Rafferty, tore down field at lightning pace. Losty, on the right, raced clean away, and reached the 21 yards mark before swinging a perfect centre in. Conlon and Kennedy pounced on it, and before Dillon realised it, the ball was in the net for the only goal of the hour. Excitement was indescribable. Placid Leinster men, who were prepared for defeat, jumped and gesticulated wildly. The ball was kicked out. Spectators were on their feet. They crowded round referee Crowe, who had refereed in a masterly way at sprinting pace, and then collapsed. Excited spectators and players stormed him with

questions, and there was a sigh of relief when a draw was announced
— Kerry, 7 points; Kildare 1:4.
     Gaelic football got a new lease of life from that wonderful drawn
game which electrified Irish sportsmen and gave the GAA a new urge in
the onward march of the nation.'

The third meeting was again in Cork, this time on 13
October 1905. M.F. Crowe again took charge of the whistle to
referee the match. The game was played on a sodden pitch in
magnificent sporting spirit. Word of the quality of the football
being served up by these two teams had spread far and wide.
Spectators flocked to the grounds to watch the final and gate
receipts of £270 broke all previous records in championship
contests. Interest was so great on this occasion that sporting fans
normally associated with rugby and soccer also made their way
to the athletic grounds to see the game.

Kerry won the thriller final by 8 points to 2 and with this
victory came a great upsurge in the status of Gaelic games in
general. The coffers of the GAA also received a much welcome
boost.

As a gesture of appreciation of the wonderful contribution
made by Kildare, the following motion, moved by T.F.
O'Sullivan of Kerry and seconded by D. O'Keeffe of Tipperary,
was unanimously passed at a meeting of the Central Council
held in Dublin on 12 November 1905: that '... the Kildare team
be presented with a set of gold medals as a souvenir of the great
home final, and in recognition of their services to the
Association'.

The 1903 All-Ireland championship home final teams were:

Kerry

T. O'Gorman (Captain), J. O'Gorman, R. Curran, Michael
McCarthy, Con Healy, Austin Stack, J. Buckley (Tralee), E. O'Neill
(Cahirciveen), Richard Fitzgerald, P. Dillon, D. McCarthy,
D. Kissane, D. Myers, W. Lynch (Killarney), P. Kirwan,
D. Breen, (Castleisland).

Kildare

J. Rafferty (Captain) (Naas), W. Merriman, L. Cribben, W. Losty,
E. Kennedy, J. Wright, J. Dunne, W. Bracken, (Clane), J. Murray,
M. Murray, M. Kennedy, J. Scott, M. Donnelly, F. Conlon,
J. Gorman, M. Fitzgerald, J. Fitzgerald (goal) (Roseberry)

On 12 November 1905, Kerry went on to defeat London Irish at Jones's Road by 11 points to 3, in the final of the 1903 All-Ireland championship.

In talking about the final of 1903, one is reminded that it was the year of the Emmet Centenary. In September, a public celebration was held in Dublin to honour the memory of Emmet — 'Bold Robert Emmet' — and the GAA had a very strong representation at the procession. The huge multitude was addressed outside St Catherine's Church, Thomas Street — the scene of Emmet's martyrdom — by the Fenian John O'Leary, who became a Patron of the GAA in 1886.

Kerry's First All-Ireland Team — 1903
*Back Row: J.P. O'Sullivan, E.J. O'Neill, D. Breen, D. Curran, D. McCarthy, M. Murray. **Second Row:** Jno. O'Gorman, J. O'Gorman, J. Myers, C. Healy, R. Kirwan, M. McCarthy, E. O'Sullivan (President Co. Board), T.F. O'Sullivan, (Hon. Sec. Co. Board). **Front Row:** W. Lynch, R. Fitzgerald, F. O'Sullivan, T. O'Gorman (Captain), P. Dillon, J.T. Fitzgerald, A. Stack. **On the Ground:** J. Buckley, L. Kissane.*

The Extra-Time Hurling Final

In 1891, only four counties from Leinster entered for the All-Ireland hurling championship. These were Wexford, Dublin, Kildare and Laois. Of these, only two actually fielded teams. Wexford's defeat of Dublin on the fourth Sunday in October, followed by a walk-over from Laois, made them Leinster champions for that year.

Neither Connaught nor Ulster put any teams forward for the inter-provincial draws that year.

In Munster, Kerry (Ballyduff) began their campaign at Killarney on 21 September when they faced Cork (Blackrock). A fit and determined Kerry team had a good win, beating Cork by 2:7 to 0:3. The calibre and ability of the Kerry team is best gauged when one calls to mind that Cork (Blackrock) went on to win the All-Ireland titles of 1893 and 1894.

In the political world, 1891 was the year of the Parnellite Split. It almost destroyed the GAA and it caused much dissension and bitterness throughout Ireland. Parnell lost many of his supporters but the 'un-crowned king of Ireland' still had a sizeable following.

The split followed confirmation of rumours of Charles Stewart Parnell's love affair with Katharine O'Shea, wife of

Captain W.H. O'Shea, a former MP Parnell was denounced by church leaders and died unexpectedly on 6 October 1891 at the age of 45. Two thousand GAA hurlers marched at his funeral. He was, after all, one of their first Patrons.

Pádraig Puirséal reported in *The Freeman* that, 'The Gaels raised their camans aloft as the coffin was borne into the City Hall and a wail arose from the people like the sound of a lonesome wind through the streets.'

T.F. O'Sullivan wrote as follows:

In the intense political excitement which prevailed throughout the country, and from which members of the organisation were not, of course, free, men's minds were turned from our national pastimes; and the terrible conflict which divided the closest personal friends, resulted in the breaking up of clubs in every county. At a representative Convention held in Dublin, the Gaels decided unanimously in favour of Mr. Parnell's leadership, and this action had the effect of alienating the support of others who were not in favour of the 'un-crowned king' retaining his position as Chairman of the Irish Party which he had created.

For a time it was feared that the Munster final between Kerry (Ballyduff) and Limerick (Treaty Stones) might not be played at all that year.

However, it did go ahead and Limerick won by 1:2 to 1:1, at Newcastle West. Kerry then lodged an objection on the grounds that time was up when Limerick scored the winning point. A replay was ordered and this time the result was decisive, but reversed, at Abbeyfeale on 31 January 1892 — Kerry 2:4; Limerick 0:1.

The All-Ireland final of 1891 took place at Clonturk on 28 February 1892. The opposing teams were Kerry (Ballyduff) and Wexford (Crossabeg). It was the last twenty-one aside final as teams were subsequently reduced to seventeen players each. It was also the last time that no number of points equalled a goal. After 1891, and up to and including 1895, a goal equalled five points. This had been decided at the Annual Convention of 1891 which was held on 13 January 1892.

Towards the close of sixty minutes, play in the 1891 final, the referee, Patrick Tobin of Dublin and Secretary of the Central Council, awarded a free to Wexford. It was taken and while the sliotar was in flight, but before it crossed for a point, the referee blew full time. Kerry claimed they had won. Wexford claimed their 'point' was the winner, but the referee said that the 'point' wasn't scored within the hour and that he had no authority to extend the time. He declared the game to be a draw at 1:1 each.

A further thirty minutes of extra time was agreed — no doubt, two periods of fifteen minutes each. The final score was Kerry 2:3; Wexford 1:5. It was Kerry's first All-Ireland hurling title and their only one to date.

T.F. O'Sullivan in *The Story of the GAA* described the game as follows: 'The match was a splendid specimen of muscular hurling. Both teams played with great dash, vigour, and determination.' Another writer said that 'these counties battled with Fianna fury and chivalry for ninety minutes.'

Kerry played in their bare feet and everyday long trousers while Wexford were described as being 'tastely dressed'.

By present-day standards it was a strange championship — only four confrontations, consisting of five games in all:

Kerry v Cork

Kerry v Limerick (Limerick's winning score disputed)

Kerry v Limerick (replay)

Wexford v Dublin

Kerry v Wexford

Two years earlier, in the championship of 1889, it was Kerry hurlers who had cause to feel aggrieved.

Kerry (Kenmare) beat Cork (Inniscara) at Mallow in the first round on 27 July. To followers of today's game, the score will be interesting — Kerry 1:1; Cork 0:5. No number of points equalled a goal and to add to Cork's dismay, the Kerry goal was scored in the last minute.

In the next round Kerry were drawn against Tipperary (Moycarkey) at Limerick Junction on Friday, 18 October. When Tipperary failed to turn up, Kerry were awarded the match. However, for some inexplicable reason the Central Council upset the decision, so it was Tipperary who went on to face and beat Clare (Tulla Emmets) who had already beaten Limerick (Liberties). However, a replay was ordered between Tipperary and Clare. Tipperary refused to replay the game and subsequently Clare were declared Munster champions — a championship in which Kerry had not been defeated.

1891 All-Ireland Senior Hurling Teams

Kerry

*J. Mahony (Captain), M. Kelly, J. Pierce, P. Carroll, P. Flanagan,
P. Wynne, M. O'Sullivan, R. Kissane, F. Crowley, P. Crowley,
J. Crowley, P. County, R. Doolan, J. O'Sullivan, T. Dunne,
P. Murphy, J. Murphy, M. Fitzsimons, J. McDonald, P. Boyle, J. Nowlan*

Wexford

N. Daly (Captain), J. Leary, E. Leary, L. Lucy, M. Lucy, Jas Murphy,
John Murphy, T. Murphy, N. Murphy, M. Browne, G. Browne,
P. Quirke, P. Byrne, M. Kirwan, M. Redmond, P. Harpur. N. Maher,
P. McDonnell. E. Daly, T. Devereux

According to T.F. O'Sullivan, the name of the other Wexford
player was not published in any of the newspaper accounts of
the match.

The following year, 1892, saw another major change in the
competition. The county champions, when representing the
county, were, if they so wished, allowed select players from
other clubs in the county.

While news on the home front was bad in 1891, there were
good things happening across the Atlantic, in America, as T.F.
O'Sullivan recorded:

*In September a convention was held in New York of delegates from all
branches of the Association in the States of Jersey and New York for the
purpose of 'devising the best means of presenting to the American public
and popularising our national sports and pastimes'. Twenty-two clubs
were represented and the Gaelic Athletic Association of America was
formally organised.*

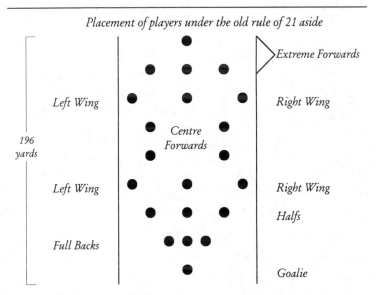

Placement of players under the old rule of 21 aside

THE PURCHASE OF CROKE PARK

In the early days of the GAA, finals were played at a variety of venues. The first All-Ireland hurling final was played in Birr and the first football final was played at the ground in Clonskeagh. At that time there wasn't a GAA General Headquarters, such as Croke Park, as there is today.

In the years following those first finals, All-Ireland title matches were played in Inchicore, Clonturk, Phoenix Park, Tipperary, Cork, Carrick-on-Suir, Dungarvan, Kilkenny, Athy and Thurles.

Finals were also played at the Jones's Road ground in Dublin. In December 1913, Jones's Road became officially known as Croke Park. The first final played there under the new title was the 1913 Football Final between Kerry and Wexford. It took place on 14 December and Kerry won by 2:2 to 0:3.

It is interesting to note, as recorded by 'Sliabh Ruadh', that for a very brief period the grounds were called Croke Memorial Park.

At Congress, held in City Hall Dublin, on Easter Sunday, 9 April 1914, with Alderman J. Nowlan in the Chair, the following resolution was passed: 'That future All Ireland Senior Championship Finals be played in Croke Memorial Park on fixed Sundays each year, one on the 1st Sunday in September, and the other on 4th Sunday in September.'

Also of interest is the background of the property and how it came to be acquired by the GAA. Here is an excerpt from an article by Paddy Downey, which appeared in *The Irish Times* on 26 July 1995:

> *...the site which Croke Park now occupies ... is part of two adjoining properties which were acquired by one owner late in the second half of the last century.*
>
> *In 1829 one of those properties, 'an orchard, dwellinghouse, yard and garden with the fields adjoining,' all containing 12 acres no roods 24*

perches was sold to one John Bradley by the Venerable John Torrens and Rev. Henry Brownrigg. Thirty five years later in 1864, Maurice Butterly bought the other plot, containing 21 acres 1 rood 12 perches from Robert Fowler. The leases of both properties were for 500 years from the dates of purchase.

As time went by the area containing the two leases was reduced by lettings for buildings and by the compulsory acquisition of portions beside the Railway wall and the Canal end by two Railway companies, Midland Great Western and Great Southern and Western.

In 1894 a newly formed company, City and Surburban Racecourse and Amusements Grounds Ltd. purchased the property, now consisting of 14 acres 0 roods 17.5 perches and for several years let the grounds for sports meetings and whippet racing as well as for Gaelic games. The first All Ireland finals played at the Jones's Road pitch were on 15th March 1896 when the hurling and football finals of 1895 were staged together on the same day.

These games resulted as follows:

Hurling — Tipperary 6:8; Kilkenny 1:0

Football — Tipperary 0:4; Meath 0:3

The first GAA event to be staged at the Jones's Road premises was the All-Ireland Track and Field championships meeting on 10 September 1892.

In every age a man of vision surfaces and it was at this point in GAA history that Frank Brazil Dinneen enters the picture. As well as being a visionary, he was an idealist and a man of integrity. He was born in 1862 in Ballylanders, County Limerick, and was a keen athlete in his youth. He grew up to be a famous one and, in 1885, he was considered the best 100-yards man in Ireland, having clocked a time of 10.6 seconds. His interest in sport continued all through his life.

He was the first President of the GAA Athletic Council. In addition, he was President of the GAA (1895–1898) and General Secretary (1898–1901) — the only man to hold both of these posts. He also served as Vice-President. 'Sliabh Ruadh' said of him, 'In the early days of the Association he took sides with the Physical Force

Frank B. Dineen

Party against the Constitutionalists, and, earlier, was imprisoned as a "suspect" under "Buckshot" Forster's regime. In 1906 he published *The Irish Athletic Record.*'

In 1893, the Association was still reeling from the shock-waves of the Parnell affair. At a Central Council meeting, held on 26 February in Thurles, Frank, then Vice-President, took the chair. He outlined to those present the depth of damage being done to the Association by the discussions on politics which were taking place at club and Central Council level. He indicated that, while the GAA would always be national in outlook, as an organisation it should divorce itself from politics and concentrate on the ideals that inspired its foundation. Happily, the response was positive and men from all sides rallied to the cause of the GAA.

In November 1908, Frank purchased the Jones's Road grounds for £3,250 plus fees, after he had tried, it would seem without success, to interest the Association in such a move. He immediately proceeded to improve the grounds. The first big match there after he took over was in April 1909 when Dublin and Tipperary met in the 1908 hurling final.

Pádraig Puirséal in his book, *The GAA and its Time*, quotes a reporter for *Sport* who commented on the improvements:

> Visitors must have rubbed their eyes in astonishment and asked themselves were they in the right place. The new Proprietor had spared neither expense nor architectural skill in the laying out of the grounds and, as an athletic arena, it is now second to none in the three kingdoms and the many that assembled must have felt sincerely proud of the Headquarters of the Gaelic Sports in Ireland. The grounds have been so arranged that, no matter how large the attendance, every individual can see the play with comfort; and as for the players, the playing pitch has been rolled and levelled so that first-class hurling is made a certainty.

In 1910, in order to fund a reduction of debts, Frank sold 4.5 acres of the grounds that lay behind the Cusack Stand side of the premises. The purchaser was the Jesuit Order which paid £1,090 and used the land as a sports field for Belvedere College. This portion of the premises was re-purchased by the GAA in 1991, before their new development of Croke Park began.

The GAA got its first great financial boost in 1913 when Kerry and Louth met on 4 May in the final of the Croke

Memorial. On a day perfect for football, 26,000 spectators were treated to a superb exhibition. 'Sliabh Ruadh' recalled the day as follows:

> Since the days of Kerry and Kildare no finer exhibition of the native code was given and the excitement and enthusiasm of the crowd was at fever point. This was the first big game played with 15 players aside and this display amply justified the change. Both teams were trained to the ounce and gave a display that established Gaelic football for all time amongst the plain people.

The game ended level — Louth 1:1; Kerry 0:4. Jack McCarthy of the Cork County Board refereed.

The replay attracted an even larger crowd — almost 50,000 — the greatest gathering ever seen up to then at Jones's Road. 'Sliabh Ruadh' wrote of this occasion:

> The game between the old rivals Kerry and Louth was a classic exhibition of Gaelic football in which the finer features of the game were displayed to advantage in spite of the sweltering heat. The crowd was enormous and thousands had to be refused admission.

With the same referee, the game finished Kerry 2:4; Louth 0:5 — 'the staying power of the Kerry men was the deciding factor.'

The teams of this historic occasion are worth recording:

Kerry

Dick Fitzgerald (Captain), D. Doyle, P. Breen, J. Skinner,
Conny Murphy, P. Healy (Killarney), Maurice McCarthy,
Tom Costelloe, J. Lawlor, D. Mullins (goal), T. Rice, P. Shea,
C. Clifford (Tralee), P. Kenneally, (Laune Rangers), J. Moriarity (Listowel)

Louth

J. Smith (Captain), J. Clarke, J. Quinn, E. Burke, L. McCormack,
P. Reilly (Fredaghs), J. Mulligan, M. Byrne (goal), J. Morgan (Young
Irelands), B. Donnelly, J. Johnson (Geraldines), O, Markey,
G. Campbell, J. Mathews (Ardee), J. Brennan (Rangers)

The total of gate receipts from these two matches came to £1,933 — £750 from the first and £1,183 from the second. This unexpected financial bonanza paved the way for the purchase of the property that was to become known as Croke Park.

In December 1913, Frank Dinneen conveyed his interest in the property, which he had purchased in 1908, to the Trustees of the GAA. He made no profit whatsoever from the transaction.

In reality, he had held the property in trust for the GAA, having viewed himself merely as a caretaker in the interim period between 1908 and 1913. The GAA's purchase was funded by a cash payment of £1,641 and the taking over of a bank debt of £2,000.

Frank, one of the great pioneers of the early days of the GAA, and nowadays a somewhat unsung hero, died in April 1916. Up to the time of his death he had been the writer of the 'Gaelic Notes' in *Sport*.

THE FOOTBALL FINAL FIASCO (1925)

In 1925, the disruption of the War of Independence and the Civil War and their immediate aftermath seemed to be finally settling down. In this more optimistic climate the GAA were looking forward to a return to normal. During the conflicts, games had been postponed and cancelled and championships had run behind schedule. Everyone hoped, that a new era was dawning.

The National Hurling and Football Leagues were established in 1925 and provision was made for non-resident players to declare for their native county. The Ban on foreign games was again debated at Congress and a motion to remove it was defeated by 69 votes to 23. Punctuality had become a major problem within the Association, so the Central Council issued a special order to all relevant bodies, indicating that teams taking the field after the appointed time would forfeit the match even if it was played and they won it.

The hurling campaign went according to plan — well, almost. The Leinster hurling final took place at Croke Park on 21 June when Dublin defeated Kilkenny by three points with a score of 6:4 to 4:7. P. McCullagh, of Wexford was the referee on this occasion. Kilkenny lodged an objection against Dublin which was based on the punctuality rule and, when it was upheld by the Leinster Council, Kilkenny were awarded the match. They subsequently fell to Galway who in turn had to give way to Tipperary in the All-Ireland final which was played on the first Sunday in September.

In the football campaign of that year much occurred that was unexpected. Indeed, by comparison, the 1911 hurling issue seemed a simple affair. The football competitions of 1925 were overshadowed by objections and counter-objections and more besides.

The story begins with the 1925 Provincial Championships. In Leinster, Wexford beat Kildare 2:7 to 0:3, to take Provincial honours for the first time since their great 'six in a row' which ended in 1918.

Kerry defeated Clare by the unusual score of 5:5 to nil, to take their third Munster title of five in a row

Cavan, then kingpins of Ulster football, were held to a draw by Antrim, 2:3 to 3 goals. However, Cavan won the replay 3:6 to 0:1, to capture their eleventh Ulster crown.

It isn't quite clear what was going on in Connaught but when it came to the semi-final the Connaught council nominated Mayo, who had been Provincial champions in 1923 and 1924, to represent the Province.

So far so good.

At Tralee on 23 August, a crowd of around 5,000 people saw Kerry gain a lucky one-point win over Cavan — 1:7 to 2:3 — in the All-Ireland semi-final.

On the same day at Croke Park, Mayo defeated Wexford in the other semi-final — just a goal between them, 2:4 to 1:4.

Then the 'fun' began.

Cavan lodged an objection against the Kerry team and Kerry filed a counter-objection. In the end, both teams were declared illegal and were suspended.

Next, Wexford made an objection against Mayo. However, the objection failed (by one vote) and Mayo were awarded the championship — but not for long.

Subsequently, Mayo lost the Connaught final to Galway by two points — a low-scoring game, 1:5 to 1:3. Following this victory, Galway were officially declared All-Ireland champions — their first senior football title ever.

Interestingly, according to 'Sliabh Ruadh' the Connaught Council who disqualified both Mayo and Galway didn't recognise Galway as the 1925 Connaught champions.

However, the matter didn't end there as Kerry sought an appeal. 'Sliabh Ruadh' in his *History of the GAA* reported as follows:

> *An important meeting of the Central Council was held on Saturday evening the 5th December, Mr P.D. Breen in the Chair. A long discussion arose regarding the All-Ireland football final, but the Chair*

(Mr. Breen) said he had ruled Galway as All-Ireland champions for 1925 and would stick to his decision. The appeal of Kerry for an All-Ireland Congress to decide the matter was turned down.

The absence of an All-Ireland final contest meant a considerable loss of revenue for the GAA. Accordingly, a gold medal tournament was arranged. As in 1910, when Kerry refused to travel and gave a walk-over to Louth in the All-Ireland final, they again refused to travel for the tournament.

On 6 December, Galway met Wexford at Croke Park and won the match by 3:4 to 1:1. They then went on to beat Cavan by 3:2 to 1:2, in the final, on 10 January 1926, at the same venue. The gold medals went to the Galway team and these wins confirmed their worthiness as All-Ireland title holders.

The Galway Victories

Connaught final: Galway 1:5; Mayo 1:3

Tournament semi-final: Galway 3:4; Wexford 1:1

Tournament final: Galway 3:2; Cavan 1:2

Like most ill winds, this football championship débâcle wasn't without its positive side. The beneficiary was Australian-born Leonard McGrath of Galway. He had won an All-Ireland hurling medal in 1923, and now through the fortunes of fate he had added a football medal. It placed him among an élite.

The GAA were glad to close the door on 1925 and look with confidence to the future.

1925 Connaught Final
Galway v Mayo

Galway line-out

M. Walsh (Captain), T. Molloy, J. Egan, D. Egan, H. Burke,
F. Benson, W. Smyth, T. Leetch, M. Bannerton, Leonard McGrath,
P. Roche, G. Jennings, P. Ganly, Lar McGrath, M. Donnellan

Writing on the affairs of the Association in 1927, 'Sliabh Ruadh' recorded the following: 'By a big majority Congress adopted the decision of the Central Council and called on the Connaught Council to hand over the medals for the 1925 Football Championship to Galway.'

1926: A Defining Moment

A Great Year for Hurling and Football and the GAA

By 1926 the benefits of peace were being felt throughout the land. Those who took the opposing views that had led, following the Treaty of 6 December 1921, to a sad, bitter and unfortunate Civil War were being slowly reconciled. Much of this reconciliation was attributable to our Gaelic games which proved to be a powerful instrument of healing.

Men once divided in the political field were now united in a sporting cause. Of course, the fact that the aims, ideals and aspirations of both sides of the conflict had much in common, aided the healing process greatly.

People were flocking to see and support our Gaelic games. The sport acted like a tonic which not only entertained and lifted spirits, but also provided a welcome intrusion and escape from daily routine. Gaelic games gave people a break from their everyday life which, in an infant economy, was for many, many people very poorly rewarded.

Here is how 'Sliabh Ruadh' summarises the year of 1926:

The year 1926 was a vintage one in GAA annals. The sun of success beamed benignly from every corner. The games were good: rivalry was keen; rigid punctuality was observed; public patronage was liberal and gate returns most flattering. The year opened well with a classic display of hurling in Cork in May between the locals and Dublin in the first final of the National hurling league. In the first round of the Leinster championship, at New Ross, another thrilling and beautiful display of the National pastime was given when Kilkenny defeated Dublin by the minimum margin. It took three games to finish the Munster final between Cork and Tipperary. The displays given were not as brilliant as the above-mentioned. Rather they were dour, dogged displays that have always been the outcome when 'Rebel Cork' and 'Gallant Tipperary' test timber and temper for the Munster hurling title.

The Central Council was incidentally lucky by having two games for the football final between the old rivals, Kerry and Kildare, the first having resulted in a draw. The dual meeting brought in a return of roughly £6,000. The Munster Council, too, had an unlooked for share of luck in the three games for the Munster hurling crown.

The tour of the Tipperary hurlers was another outstanding event in the GAA annals. The tour was a splendid success and happy results were achieved. The splendid displays of the Tipperary men thrilled thousands of our exiled countrymen and also brought splendid patronage from the American sporting public. The first National leagues were also concluded this year and fully justified their initiation. Cork won the hurling from Dublin, and Leix won the football from the same county. For the All Ireland hurling final, Cork had revenge after fourteen years over their old rivals, Kilkenny, before a concourse of twenty six thousand at Croke Park; and in football Kerry won the championship from Kildare.

Altogether the year 1926 was an outstanding one in GAA annals, and the historians of the future can mark down this year as the beginning of a great cycle in the history of our National Athletic Association.

The *Kilkenny Journal* commented as follows:

In general administration, in the carrying out of fixtures, in punctuality and public patronage, in the cleanliness and high standard of the games themselves, there has been a distinct advance, so that the year 1926 will go down in history as the greatest year so far in the annals of the Association.

In Munster, Cork qualified for the final with very easy wins over both Waterford and Kerry.

Meanwhile Tipperary, All-Ireland champions of 1925, arrived back at Cobh from the United States on the evening of Sunday, 24 July. They returned to Ireland victorious after a memorable coast to coast tour of the US where they played, and convincingly won, seven games in all.

The results make interesting reading:

New York, 30 May 1926
Tipperary — 11:4; Offaly (Champions of New York State) — 2:2

Boston, 31 May 1926
Tipperary — 9:5; Cork (Selection New York) — 4:1

Chicago 6 June 1926
Tipperary — 7:10; Chicago (Selection) — 3:2

San Francisco 13 June 1926:
Tipperary — 10:4; California (Selection)— 5:2

Buffalo 20 June 1926:
Tipperary — 16:6; Buffalo (Selection) — 4:3
Chicago 27 June 1926:
Tipperary — 12:3; Chicago (Selection) — 2:3
New York 11 July 1926:
Tipperary — 10:4 New York (Selected) — 3:2

On 21 August, Tipperary met Limerick in a tough, gruelling game which was well controlled by referee Paddy O'Keeffe — it was only one of many such clashes between the counties in those years.

'Sliabh Ruadh's' comments on the 1922 Munster final captures the action and atmosphere of these clashes:

> *The replay of the Munster Hurling Final between Tipperary and Limerick took place on Sunday, 12 August, at Limerick before a crowd of 20,000. The previous game at Thurles on 1 July resulted in a draw of 2:2 each. Sunday's gate receipts totalled £1363, and the contest will rank as the most Homeric encounter recorded in the annals of the game. The pace was terrific and the casualty list abnormal. Final scores Tipp. 4:2 Limerick 1:4.*

However, back to 1926. In a match of no quarter, Tipperary had a somewhat lucky win, taking two goals towards the end of the game for a final result of 6:5 to 4:6 — and so securing a place in the final against Cork.

It took three meetings to decide the issue. The first was a fiasco when the two teams faced each other at Cork Athletic grounds. The crowd, estimated to be in excess of thirty thousand, far exceeded the capacity of the venue. Referee Dinny Lanigan, of Limerick, had to call the game off after twenty minutes. Tipperary were leading 1:2 to nil, when the crowd spilled onto the pitch after the barriers gave way under pressure.

A week later, on 19 September, Tipperary and Cork met again, this time at Thurles. Under the guidance of Tom Semple, preparations were made which ensured that there would be no repeat of the previous Sunday's events. This time Cork took the early initiative and even though they led by 2:3 to 1 goal at the break, it finished all square at 3:4 to Tipperary's 4:1.

The replay took place on 3 October, at the same venue where a crowd of around 30,000 was treated to a hectic encounter, full of thrills and excitement. With a final score 3:6 to 2:4, Cork had dethroned the champions. Their supporters, who had not seen an All-Ireland win since 1919, and before that since 1903, went wild with enthusiasm.

However, the hurling classic of the year belonged to Leinster. It took place at New Ross on 30 May between Kilkenny and Dublin. With Sean O'Kennedy of Wexford as referee, a crowd of twelve thousand people gathered to watch the match and a close, fast, superb exhibition of the game held them spellbound. The wizardry of Lory (Meagher) was to the fore, as recounted in *Giants of the Ash* and *Hurling Giants*. The final whistle blew with Kilkenny a point to the good, beating Dublin by 4:8 to 5:4 in what had been a breathtaking contest.

In 1926 alone, one could pick more than one team of the century from the ranks of Kilkenny, Dublin, Cork, Limerick, Galway and Tipperary — the stars were legion and the names legendary.

Football too was a champion of Gaelic games in 1926. The final showdown was between Kerry and Kildare who had not met in a final since 1905 when Kildare had won by 1:7 to Kerry's 0:5.

Once again an All-Ireland final was not settled first time out, and on 5 September the game ended in a draw — Kerry 1:3; Kildare 0:6. The replay on 17 October attracted what was, for then, a huge crowd of roughly forty thousand people. A total of fifty trains converged on the capital and gate receipts totalled £3,370. The great names of the day adorned the scene — among them, from Kildare: Larry Stanley, Matt Goff, Jack Higgins, Joe Loughlin, Paul Doyle, Gus Fitzpatrick and Bill Gannon; and from Kerry: John Joe Sheehy, Joe Barrett, Jack Walsh, Paul Russell and Con Brosnan.

Comments on the game were as follows:

Staged amid a setting unrivalled, unapproached, unprecedented in the annals of Gaelic activity, the great final for Irish football honours for 1926 will go down in history as the greatest yet played.

Tense excitement, brilliant football, orderly appreciative thousands, all aided by ideal weather, favoured the great fixture.

Kerry's triumph, the outcome of the 'Kingdom's' traditional dash, was superior only in victory to the defiant defence of the Short Grass

County that, with victory within sight, tasted defeat with a dignity
worthy of the best traditions of the Gael.

The final score was Kerry 1:4; Kildare 0:4 — Kerry's seventh All-Ireland crown.

The National leagues had a good start that year. The football league was based on six divisions, with Sligo emerging at the top in Connaught, while Antrim were leaders in Ulster. In Munster, Kerry won through and, from the three divisions in Leinster, Longford, Dublin and Leix headed the tables.

In the draw that followed, Sligo, Dublin and Leix had victories over Longford (3:1 to 0:5), Antrim (0:8 to 0:5) and Kerry (1:6 to 1:5) respectively. After that, Leix were drawn against Sligo and beat them after a replay by 4:6 to 1:4.

On 19 September they met Dublin in the final at New Ross and won by 2:1 to 1 goal.

The hurling competition was run on a direct league basis. Seven teams — Cork, Dublin, Leix, Tipperary, Galway, Limerick and Kilkenny competed in the first division. The first hurling league tie was played at Cashel on 4 October 1925 when Kilkenny defeated Tipperary by 5:2 to 3:1. Cork won five of their six games — losing only to Leix — and headed the table with a total of ten points. Their win over Dublin — runners up with eight points — in their last game of the series decided the destination of the first league title.

Excitement in the crowd at the drawn game at Thurles — Tipperary 3:4; Cork 4:1. Courtesy *Tipperary Star*

A second division comprised Clare, Offaly, Kerry, Waterford and Wexford. Clare topped the table, winning all four games while Offaly came second with three wins, losing only to Clare. Waterford and Wexford — over whom Kerry registered wins — lost all four of their games.

In 1927, the Central Council decided to run only one hurling division which was to consist of Tipperary, Cork, Limerick, Clare, Galway, Kilkenny, Dublin, Leix and Offaly.

At this time, Central Council also divided the football league into three divisions.

So, with Championships well established, National Leagues in place, Railway Cup competitions about to emerge, and attendance at the All-Ireland Football final exceeding the figure for Rugby Internationals for the first time ever, the GAA was certainly well on the march — and marching on to success and glory.

THE POINT-LESS HURLING TITLE

The duel was a dour one, keen and manly

The winter of 1910 saw a unique meeting between Wexford (Castlebridge) and Limerick (Castleconnell) in the All-Ireland senior hurling final. The Wexford team was captained by Dick Doyle, while John 'Tyler' Mackey led Limerick. The match was played at Jones's Road on 20 November.

This was the first time in twenty years that none of the 'Big Three' — Tipperary, Cork and Kilkenny —were contesting the final. Wexford, who wore blue jerseys with yellow shoulders, were contesting their fourth final. Up to that time they were without success, having lost to Cork in 1890 and to Kerry, after extra time, in 1891— the only time ever that extra time was played in a final (up to the time of publication of this book, in 1999). They lost the final again in 1899, to Tipperary.

Limerick on the other hand, who wore green with gold hoops, had been successful in their only All-Ireland appearance when they defeated Kilkenny in 1897, by 3:4 to 2:4.

The 1910 final saw the introduction of some rule changes. A parallelogram, often referred to as 'the square', was drawn in front of each goal, five yards deep by fifteen yards across. To be present in that area before the arrival of the sliotar meant that an ensuing goal would be disallowed. Understandably, players found it difficult to re-adjust to the changes and even the interpretations by officials, especially a visiting American umpire, caused much confusion. Limerick had three goals disallowed. Wexford had one.

The sideposts through which points could be scored were also abolished. A 'seventy' was introduced instead of a 'fifty' and goal nets were also provided.

The attendance was in the region of 10,000 people and, for the first time, sideline seats in the form of chairs were available. The basic charge to the grounds was six old pence (two and a half new pence) and total gate receipts amounted to £288. It had been the custom to admit ladies free up to that time, but demand was such that the practice was discontinued at the 1910 final.

In the first round Limerick had beaten Clare, on 22 May, and followed up with a 6:3 to 3:0 win over Kerry on 2 October. Meanwhile, Cork beat defending Munster champions, Tipperary, on 3 July, in Limerick, by 5:7 to 3:4. The Munster final in Tralee, on 16 October, produced the surprise of the year, with Limerick stunning a highly confident Cork fifteen, taking the victory with a final score of 5:1 to 4:2.

In Leinster, Kilkenny, the All-Ireland champions, fell to Dublin, on 11 September, at Portlaoise. Many may find it strange to learn that Dublin's next game was against Glasgow. In the early years of the century, efforts were made to involve the Gaels of Glasgow, and indeed of Scotland, in our games (as had been done for those in London). Success was quite limited, however.

'Sliabh Ruadh' records that in 1909:

> During the month of July the Glasgow Raparee Hurling Club toured the South of Ireland and played matches with some of the Cork and Tipperary teams, notably the Lahorna De Wetts and Midleton. The object of the tour was to raise funds to enable the Gaels of Glasgow to purchase a field solely for Gaelic Games.

In 1910, he further noted the following:

> After an absence of four years the Gaels of Scotland fielded a team against an Ulster selection at the Gaelic Grounds, Belfast, in the All-Ireland championship. The visitors out-classed their opponents and the final scores were Scotland 1:13; Ulster 7 points.

In the event, Dublin beat Glasgow, 6:6 to 5:1. Meanwhile, Wexford disposed of Offaly, by 5:12 to 1:7, in the first round of the Leinster championship. They then went on to defeat Dublin by 3:3 to 1:1, in the final at Athy, on 30 October. This win caused as big a surprise in GAA circles as had Limerick's victory over Cork.

Earlier in the year, Wexford had beaten Cork in a tournament game played at Dungarvan. Everything, therefore, pointed to a close and stirring contest in the final between Wexford and Limerick; and so it proved to be.

Huge crowds travelled from Wexford and Limerick on the day of the final. They witnessed a hard, hectic, uncompromising physical battle between two fit, and well-prepared sides. Wexford's excellent teamwork, especially in the first half when they kept pushing forward in waves, set them on the road to victory. Dick Doyle was their top scorer.

Limerick's rally in the second half almost saved the day for them. They dominated the game and, with seven minutes remaining, were within a point of Wexford. It was now anybody's game. Excitement became intense as the men from Garryowen launched some fierce attacks. A very promising attack ended in a wide, and the opportunity for Limerick to draw or win was lost.

In the course of writing my first book, *Giants of the Ash*, I visited the late Mick Neville, in Castlebridge in 1981. He was 94 years old at the time and had attended the Wexford *v* Cork All-Ireland final of 1976. (He had spent his life as a postman and when he retired, at 75 years of age, he reckoned he had covered a distance of over 80,000 miles. Unfortunately, after sixty years' service his grade didn't qualify him for a pension. In retirement, he turned to his favourite hobby, gardening, and won many awards for his exhibits at shows.)

Mick still has very clear memories of the 1910 All-Ireland final:

> *We played seventeen aside; seven down the centre and five on each of the wings. I was marking John Madden. It was nearly all ground hurling and hard pulling. We scored a goal in the opening minutes. The pace was very fast. I found the roar of the crowd terrifying. I had never before played before such a large crowd. Then Limerick got a point and a goal. After that we got a goal when Egan Clancy of Limerick was down injured. In those days play was stopped when a player went down. Most of us stopped playing and one of our lads tipped the ball into the net. I didn't think it would be allowed but it was. We led by 6 goals to 3:1 at half-time.*
>
> *When the final whistle blew I didn't know who had won. I knew it was close. But with scores being disallowed and argued about, I didn't know what way it was.*

The final score was 7:0 to 6:2 in Wexford's favour and thus they captured their first crown. Excluding London, who won the title in 1901, Wexford were the seventh county to add their name to the honours list. At that time their outstanding player was Sean O'Kennedy, at full back, who thwarted many a Limerick effort. He was ably supported by Dick Fortune, Sim Donohoe, Paddy Mackey and Dick Doyle. All were heroes of the game. Sean O'Kennedy subsequently captained Wexford to All-Ireland football fame in 1915, 1916 and 1917. Kilkenny-born Paddy Mackey was also on the victorious Wexford hurling team. He too was a brilliant footballer and won a total of four All-Ireland football medals with Wexford, in the years 1915–1918 inclusive.

The All-Ireland final of 1910 was the first and only time to date that the winners failed to score a point. The abolition of the side posts no doubt contributed to this. (A look at the scoring records prior to 1910 shows that points were a main feature of games up to that time, while, subsequent to 1910, points were scarce for a number of years until players got used to the new system.) This very sporting All-Ireland final was refereed by Michael Crowe, a Limerick man resident in Dublin. He was a noted and respected referee and this was his fifth time officiating at an All-Ireland hurling final.

Immediately after the final whistle, and on hearing the score (which he couldn't believe) the Limerick captain, 'Tyler' Mackey, lodged an objection, claiming that Limerick had won. Days later, the Limerick County Board followed up with their objection, the basis of which was 'incompetent umpiring'. The Central Council, however, refused to uphold the objection which was not, it appears, submitted in accordance with the rules. Accordingly, the result stood.

Wexford were worthy All-Ireland champions at their fourth attempt.

1910 All-Ireland Hurling Final

Wexford

(Selection from Castlebridge, Screen, New Ross and Oulart).
Dick Doyle (Captain), Dave Kavanagh, Mike Cummins, Andy Keogh,
W. McHugh, Jim Shortal, Paddy Mackey, Sim Donohoe,
Pat Corcoran, Mick Neville, Michael Parker, Jas Mythen, Dick Fortune,
Sean O'Kennedy, William Devereux, Jas Fortune, Pat Roche (goal)

Limerick

(Selection from Castleconnell, Fedamore, Croom, Young Irelands,
Rathkeale, Commercials and Boher)
Mick Danaher, John 'Tyler' Mackey (Captain), M. Sweeney,
Dave Conway, Sean O'Carroll, Ned Treacy, Con Scanlon,
Egan Clancy, Mick Harrington, Mick Mangan, Mick Feely,
Ter Mangan, Tim O'Brien, Tom Hayes, Paddy Flaherty, John Madden,
J. Bourke (goal)

Sean O'Kennedy

Goal-Scoring Areas

Before 1910

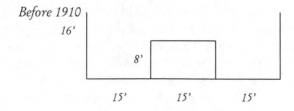

1910 and after

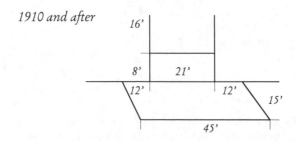

THE DAY JACK LYNCH WON HIS FOOTBALL MEDAL

Where we sported and played, 'neath each green leafy glade,
On the banks of my own lovely Lee

It was a sunny Sunday morning and we were on our way home from 8.30 Mass in my native parish of Ardagh, in West Limerick. People were talking about the football final, as indeed they had been for most of the previous week. Central to the discussion was not whether Cork or Cavan would win, but whether Jack Lynch would win his fifth All-Ireland medal in a row.

A great Cork hurling era had seen them win four successive hurling titles, from 1941 to 1944, and Jack had played in each of the finals. On this day, everyone was wondering if he could win a football medal and join a small élite of successful, dual hurling and football medal-winning players. Time would tell.

It all made for good friendly discussion and everyone seemed to be an expert, even though they didn't all hold the same view. Still though, there were those whom I felt knew what they were talking about and I kept reflecting on what they had said.

Money was very scarce in those days. Pennies were hard to come by — for four pence you could go to the pictures at matinée time; for six pence you could buy a big bottle of lemonade. As we sat down to dinner, I approached my father and said I would bet him six pence that Cork would win. He was a native of North Longford and as a child had only to cross a few fields, from his family's farm, to get to County Cavan. I felt he couldn't refuse to back a close neighbour and he didn't. I eagerly awaited the final whistle.

Down in Cork, the football record was being scrutinised, but it wasn't great. Back in the last century they had won the 1890 title — a twenty-one aside affair — with a win over Wexford at Clonturk (the game was played on 26 June 1892). The Cork hurlers had made it an 1890 All-Ireland double when, in an unfinished game against Wexford, they were awarded the title.

In 1911, Cork had taken a second football All-Ireland title with a decisive win over Antrim by 6:6 to 1:2 — this time in a seventeen-aside match. However, in 1928, a victory in Munster was followed by a heavy defeat at the hands of a great Kildare team in the All-Ireland semi-final. Fifteen years passed before Cork won in Munster again. However, on 15 August 1943, the future began to look brighter for Cork in a thrilling semi-final with Cavan. Cork, with Jack Lynch very much to the fore, lost by only one point — 1:8 to 1:7.

Such was Cork's footballing history up to 1945. The question now was whether they could win a third title and a first in a fifteen-aside final. Cork's path to the final read as follows:

v *Tipperary* — 1:7 to 1:6

v *Kerry* — 1:11 to 1:6

v *Galway* — 2:12 to 2:8

Jeremiah A. Beckett

The All-Ireland football final of 1945 was no easy game for either side. Led by Tadhg Crowley, Cork were a seasoned outfit. Cavan, on the other hand, were without their brilliant half-forward Mick Higgins. Even so, could Cork undo the semi-final result of 1943 and repeat the All-Ireland success of 1911?

For those who believed in omens, the portents were good for Cork. There were encouraging links with the victorious 1911 team. Both Jack Young and Jeremiah A. Beckett had played then and, in 1945, each had a son on the Cork team; midfielder, Eamon Young and corner-forward, Derry Beckett.

The ball was thrown in by GAA President Seamus Gardiner, of Tipperary, and, from then until the final whistle, it was a close hard-fought game. The crowd of 70,000 spectators were kept in a state of constant excitement right up to the last five minutes when a Derry Beckett goal sealed victory for Cork. The final ended on the score of Cork 2:5; Cavan 0:7. Each team had taken seven scores, but the deciding factor was that two of Cork's were goals. Interestingly, nearly all of the Cork scores came from the left-wing opportunists Derry Beckett and Mick Tubridy. Mick was a Clare man and an Army man — an athlete of great speed — who later declared for Clare and was also famous as a member of the Irish Equestrian team. Left full back, on the Cork team, was Caleb Crone who had won an All-Ireland medal in the same position with Dublin in 1942.

The win also enabled Derry Beckett to join the list of All-Ireland dual medal winners, as he had already won a hurling medal with Cork in 1942. His father, Jeremiah, was denied a hurling medal in 1905 following a Kilkenny objection that led to a replay which was lost by Cork. Only for that Kilkenny victory, the Beckett family would have had a unique father and son double. Jeremiah had also come close to a hurling medal in the 1907 All-Ireland championship. The final was played at Dungarvan on 21 June 1908, when, in an unforgettable hurling classic, Cork lost by just one point to Kilkenny — 3:12 to 4:8.

Jeremiah, a hard man on the field, was a fine athlete — sprinter, hurler, footballer, referee — and was long-puck champion in 1909, with a 93-yards drive; he was also the Irish 220-yards champion, in 1910. During his days in Dublin, he played with Keatings and Erin's Hope and it isn't widely known that Jeremiah was, in fact, a Kerryman. He hailed from Kilgarvan in South Kerry — a parish that has always had a hurling tradition. When he became a teacher he moved to Cork. It is surely a little ironic, that his grandson, Jeremiah, is now a doctor in County Kilkenny — the county that denied his grandfather that All-Ireland hurling medal in 1905.

However, back to Jack Lynch. Many years after the 1945 final, I met him, when I was working on my book, *Giants of the Ash*, in 1981, and then again in 1983, at an All-Stars Banquet. By that time he had played in seven successive All-Ireland finals and won six successive All-Ireland medals — 1941–1944 in hurling, 1945 in football and

Derry Beckett

Jack Lynch

again in hurling in 1946. Cork had lost by one point to Kilkenny in 1947.

I told Jack that he was the topic of much discussion in our locality and household in 1945. I also told him about my bet of sixpence, to which he replied: 'That was a lot of money in those days', followed by, 'Your judgement was sound — did you collect?' I confirmed that I did. Jack's great record in All-Ireland finals wasn't his only remarkable achievement on the fields of Gaelic games. In 1944, on Sunday, 20 February, he played a Dublin senior hurling league game for Civil Service against Eoghan Ruadh in the morning, and lost. In the afternoon, he played for Munster against Ulster, in hurling, and this time his team won by 9:3 to 3:1. He also played for Munster in the football game against Ulster which was lost 2:10 to 1:7. Jack is reported to have scored in all three games. In an interview, when the matter came up for discussion, Jack said that he certainly wouldn't recommend three games in any one day.

Jack related an amusing incident to me that happened as he made his way to Croke Park on football final day, 1945. He decided to take the bus, so he joined the queue at a bus stop in the city. The buses were passing by, either because they were full or because they were taking on only a few passengers, depending on the amount of seats available. It was pushing on towards match time and Jack was getting anxious. The next bus pulled up and when Jack realised he wasn't going to get a seat, he approached the conductor and explained that he was playing that day with Cork in the football final and that 'twas important he should get to Croke Park on time. The bus conductor looked at him disbelievingly and told him it was a good story — 'I haven't heard that one before — sorry, no room.'

Eventually, Jack did get to Croke Park, and inside the dressing-room, someone said to him: 'You're great to come!'

The winning team of that year read as follows:

Moll O'Driscoll (Clonakilty)
Dave Magnier (Fermoy), Weeshie Murphy (Beara)
Caleb Crone (Air Corps)
Paddy Cronin (Fermoy), Tadhg Crowle y (Captain) (Clonakilty),
Din O'Connor (Millstreet)
Fachtna O'Donovan(Clonakilty), Eamon Young (Army)
'Togher' Casey (Clonakilty), Humphrey O'Neill (Clonakilty),
Mick Tubridy (Army)
Jack Lynch (St Nicholas's), Jim Cronin (Army)
Derry Beckett (St Finbarr's)

Subs: Brendan Murphy (Beara), Sean Kavanagh (Commercials),
Mick Finn (Clonakilty), Dessie Cullinane (Clonakilty),
Paddy (Hitler) Healy (Clonakilty), David Roche (Fermoy),
Paddy O'Grady (Fermoy), Sean Lenihan (St Nicholas),
Tadhg O'Driscoll (Fermoy).

Paddy D. Mehigan (Carbery), himself a Corkman, was at Croke Park to relish Cork's great win after their lapse of thirty-four years. He celebrated by composing a ballad to the air of 'Agus Fagfaimid siud Mar atá Sé':

'Twas up in Croke Park on last Sunday I hear
That the Corkmen faced Cavan whose fame was so dear;
Those Northerners were good and our scores they ran near,
But we held them and led them and beat them.
'Twas Beckett's grand goal that finished the fray,
And Tubridy's pace was the talk of the day,
But our backs were like granite where Weeshy held sway
Agus fagfaimid siud mar atá sé.

Brave Crone and Dave Magnier from sweet old Fermoy,
Din Cronin, Pat Connor, our pride and our joy,
Ross-Fachna O'Donovan, ranging and coy,
And where would you leave Eamon Young, boys?
He dummied and drove like his father of old,
And showed them some tricks from Dunmanway, I'm told,
Humphrey Neill and Jack Lynch and Jim Cronin so bold
Set our heroes like beagles in tongue, boys.

'Tocher' Casey was marking his man near the hour —
Hand and foot he kept dodging, then driving with power,
Macroom and Millstreet and Cork town; but the flower
Were Weeshy and Crowley our captain.
So here's to our footballers fearless and free,
Clonakilty, Rosscarbery and famed Dunmanway,
The Sam Maguire Cup has come home to the Lee
Agus fagfaimid siud mar atá sé.

It was a great win for Cork and a memorable day for Jack
Lynch. Yet, hurling was his first love as this extract from a
speech he made at a Symposium on hurling organised by Na
Piarsigh GAA Club, Limerick, on 28 May 1968, clearly
indicates:

Hurling is far more than a game — it is almost a way of life — it is an
all-engrossing physical, mental and, indeed, cultural exercise, because the
hurler becomes wrapped up in the rich tradition of the game, becomes
identified with an art which is distinctly and uniquely Irish in origin
and development. The true hurler is a man of dignity, proud of his
heritage, skilful, well-disciplined, and a sportsman.

Every game has its good points, and every player will, naturally, tend
to claim that the game he favours is the best. I have tried my hand at a
number of them in my time — football, handball, tennis, golf — but for
me, as for the vast majority of others who have experienced the different
thrills of these differing games, there is nothing to equal the thrills of a good
hurling game. There is nothing to equal the satisfying experience of
connecting with a sliotar in mid-air and sending it onwards with
accelerated speed, or the clean clash of camáns in a hip-to-hip encounter
with an opponent, or the beauty of a ball rising straight and true over the
bar from a side-line cut-in or a 70. The speedy ebb and flow of play, the
skills and excitement of the game are the big attractions for the player and
the spectator alike. And this is one of the most important aspects of the
game in the National life of the country — it is an expression of all that is
vigorous and skilful, artistic and exciting in our nature. It would be a
national tragedy if we were to allow such a truly representative symbol of
Irish character to fade away. Looking at hurling from a National view-
point, and recognising it for what it is — the fastest and one of the finest
field-games in the world and Ireland's very special contribution to the
world of sport — one cannot but wonder to what extremes of endeavour
other countries, such as the United States, England, France, Germany,
would go to promote it if it were their very special and unique National
game. And one is prompted to ask if Ireland is less proud of her cultural
heritage, less proud of her greatest game than those countries are of theirs.

There was an amusing aspect to my first meeting with Jack in 1981. It took place, by appointment, at Dáil Éireann.

I kept wondering what way I would address him. It would be our first meeting. He didn't know me but I knew him well. Ever since 1945 he was, to me, Jack — Jack Lynch, Cork hurler and footballer.

Would I address him as Jack? I would like to, but I had doubts. It mightn't be right. How I wished he was still Taoiseach — I would have felt comfortable with Taoiseach but that option didn't now exist.

What about Mr? No way. That was out of the question. Mr Lynch would be ridiculous; I'd be talking to a stranger if I said Mr Lynch — I decided to play it by ear.

I was taken to his office by a very charming lady who enquired if I had ever seen him play. 'Only through the eyes and voice of Mícheál O'Hehir,' I had had to confess.

A most pleasant meeting ensued. And how did I address him? I avoided the matter completely. Unwittingly, Jack made up my mind for me. As I entered his office, there was a friendly handshake accompanied by, 'You're welcome, Mr Fullam'. That did it. And in that moment, how I wished that Jack — Jack Lynch — was still Taoiseach.

LIAM MacCARTHY

Liam MacCarthy was born in England in 1853, his parents having emigrated from Ireland, following eviction two years before. His father, Eoghan, was a native of Ballygarvan, County Cork. His mother, Brigid Dineen, a renowned Irish dancer, hailed from Bruff, County Limerick. At the time of Liam's birth his father was 21 years old and his mother was aged 29.

In 1875, Liam married Alice Padbury, daughter of a London businessman, and for some time he worked in his in-laws' business as a supervisor. Prior to that, he had initially been a blacksmith's hammer man and then a railway-signal fitter.

As Liam grew to manhood he matured into a mighty man — over six foot in height and weighing 18 stone — with a huge frame. Not surprisingly, he was described as a horse of a man.

When his mother died in 1877, aged 53, Liam was distraught — a very special bond had existed between them. From his mother he had inherited a deep love of Ireland and all things Irish — its politics, history, language and mythology — and as a result, he never forgot his roots. He had treasured her guidance and counsel and her death left a terrible void.

From his father he inherited discipline, organisational ability and a strong sense of duty; but the relationship between them didn't match that of Liam and his mother.

In 1890, his father died, at which time Liam had established his own cardboard box-manufacturing business — a trade he had learned with his in-laws. As it progressed and developed, he formed a company called William MacCarthy and Sons Cardboard Box Factory, at Haymerle Road, Peckham, London. His affection for his mother is reflected in the fact that he called the factory St Brigid's Works, in memory of her.

Liam's level of mental and physical energy were such that he was able to be actively involved in a wide range of diverse activities.

- He participated in the St Vincent de Paul and Legion of Mary.

- He was vice-president of the Gaelic League. His love for the Irish language was such that he gave significant financial support to Pádraig Pearse's School, St Enda's.

- He was associated with the promotion of Gaelic games and was active in GAA affairs in London from the start. He also gave generous financial support to the Association.

- When the London County Board was formed, in 1896, Liam was elected its first Treasurer and for twelve years he acted as referee at hurling games.

- He was President of the London County Board from 1898 to 1907. He was succeeded by Sam Maguire but returned to the post from 1909 to 1911.

- His love of Ireland saw him and his son, Eugene, become members of the IRB. Basically a man of peace, Liam's preferred road to freedom would have been a constitutional one. Loss of life disturbed him.

- He was elected Councillor to the Borough of Camberwell for North Peckham, No. 7 Ward, in 1900, and remained on the Council for 12 years.

- In 1903 he was made Manager of St Francis's Roman Catholic School.

His love for hurling was immense and whenever he visited Ireland he would return with a bundle of hurleys. It is hardly surprising that he should have decided to donate a trophy for the All-Ireland Senior Hurling Championship. The new trophy was made in Dublin to Liam's design. The cost at the time was £50 — surely the equivalent of about £3,500 in today's money.

The first winners of the Liam MacCarthy Cup were Limerick in the All-Ireland championship of 1921. They were captained by Bob McConkey and the final was played on 4 March 1923.

In 1992, after seventy years of service, the Liam MacCarthy Cup was replaced. Bhí a seal tugtha. The last man to receive the cup was Tipperary Captain Declan Carr, in 1991. It is now displayed in the Croke Park Museum.

Liam Fennelly, of Kilkenny, has a personal record all his own where the Liam MacCarthy Cup is concerned. In 1983, when Kilkenny won their twenty-third All-Ireland title, he returned to the Noreside with the original cup. Nine years later, in 1992, Kilkenny won their twenty-fourth All-Ireland title. Liam was captain again, and so he collected the new MacCarthy Cup — the first man to do so. In so doing, he became the only captain in the history of the Association to have been presented with both cups.

Nine captains received the hurling trophy more than once — Sean Óg Murphy for Cork, 1926, 1928; Jimmy Walsh for Kilkenny, 1932, 1939; Mick Mackey for Limerick, 1936, 1940; Christy Ring for Cork, 1946, 1953, 1954; Nick O'Donnell Wexford, 1955, 1960; Jimmy Doyle for Tipperary, 1962, 1965; Conor Hayes for Galway, 1987, 1988; Liam Fennelly for Kilkenny, 1983, 1992 and Anthony Daly for Clare, 1995, 1997.

To date, 1999, ten counties have won the Liam MacCarthy Cup:

County	Titles	County	Titles
Kilkenny	18	Cork	21
Wexford	5	Tipperary	15
Offaly	4	Limerick	5
Dublin	3	Clare	2
Galway	4	Waterford	2

All hurling fans look forward to the day when a team from Ulster will capture the Liam MacCarthy Cup.

Liam, a teetotaller all his life, who was in failing health from 1906 onwards, died on 28 September 1928. He was buried in an unmarked grave.

Through the efforts of John Meaney, co-author with Damian Gaffney of *Ireland's Forgotten Son — The Liam MacCarthy Story*, which provided much of the detail for this chapter, Liam's grave was located in Dulwich.

John Meaney's employer, the *Irish World* newspaper in Britain funded the cost and erection of a headstone at the grave site. At Easter 1996, on the occasion of the centenary of the London County Board, the headstone was unveiled before a distinguished gathering.

John Meaney spoke these words at the graveside:

Here lies a great Irishman.

Liam MacCarthy was born in London of Irish parents and carried his Irishness with great pride at a time when it was not popular to do so.

At the turn of the century, Liam MacCarthy was involved in helping Irish people to relocate in London, by finding accommodation and work for them.

As a Councillor, he worked tirelessly to ensure that they retained their heritage through politics and sport.

Liam became known as the Father of the GAA in London and spent ten years leading the London County Board, helping to create the vibrant organisation that we enjoy today.

He worked with highly acclaimed Irishmen like Sam Maguire, Michael Collins and Patrick Pearse.

Through determination and dedication, he helped carve and shape the Irish community in London.

We are now reaping the benefits of his outstanding achievements.

It is right and fitting that we honour this great Irishman in this historic year for the GAA as they celebrate their Centenary and hold their first ever Congress in London.

Let us make today's service a platform for a new beginning, re-awakening the unity and trust achieved by the efforts of Liam MacCarthy all those years ago.

He brought strength, companionship and respect to an Irish community in its infancy.

Liam was known as Fighting Mac, because he was at the forefront of every cause that needed to be fought for the Irish at a very sensitive time in our history.

He was a man of great character, proud of his Irish roots and the best way we can honour his memory is to work together to create a new Irishness, one of Justice, Unity and above all one of Peace.

Here lies a truly great Irishman.

Liam MacCarthy

SAM MAGUIRE

The name of Sam Maguire is immortalised in the All-Ireland Senior Football trophy which was presented to the GAA by his friends and admirers. Its design and shape replicate the world famous Ardagh Chalice, though the trophy is larger in size.

Sam was born in Dunmanway, County Cork. He was of the Protestant persuasion and was one of the few of his faith to join the GAA, unlike the Gaelic League which attracted many non-Catholics.

He was an excellent Gaelic footballer and was a dedicated upholder of the ideals of the GAA. He was always closely associated with the Irish teams in London, from his arrival there in 1899, and played for London in the finals of 1900, against Tipperary; 1901 against Dublin; and in 1903 against Kerry. Unfortunately for the exiles, they lost all three matches. Sam was captain of the London team in 1901 and 1903 and was also President of the London County Board for a number of years.

He was also actively involved in politics and the Republican movement. It was Sam Maguire who swore Michael Collins into the IRB. An article in *An tÓglach* (Easter 1965), edited by Piaras Béaslaí, contained the following:

> *Sam Maguire held the rank of Major General and was Chief Intelligence Officer in Britain. He was a born underground and enemy-resistance leader. He broke through all barriers of the highest British Intelligence Departments to get vital information, of the utmost value to the IRA at home, which often saved them from falling into dangerous situations. He was not known to Scotland Yard although he worked under their noses in the P.O. Sorting Office, Mount Pleasant, London. Secret enquiries had been circulated to Police stations and Intelligence Agencies all over England to trace 'S.M.' and Sam was laughing with copies of them in his pocket as he went complacently about his business.*

However, his luck ran out and British Intelligence eventually caught up with him. He was imprisoned for gun-running between London and Dublin; he was, of course, sacked from his job.

Sam Maguire died in 1927 and is buried in his native West Cork.

The first winners of the Sam Maguire trophy were Kildare, in 1928. They defeated Cavan, with a last-minute point, by 2:6 to 2:5, and their captain, Bill 'Squire' Gannon, collected the cup. The game was refereed by Alderman T. Burke of Drogheda.

In 1960, Kevin Mussen, Down's right half back and captain, was the first man to take the Sam Maguire Cup across the Border.

Fourteen counties, representing all four provinces, have won the Sam Maguire Cup. The honours list is as follows:

Ulster
Down 5, Cavan 5, Donegal 1, Derry 1

Connaught
Galway 7, Mayo 3, Roscommon 2

Munster
Kerry 24, Cork 4

Leinster
Dublin 8, Meath 6, Offaly 3, Kildare 1, Louth 1

It is interesting to note that two counties from Northern Ireland, Down and Derry, have been successful in taking the Sam Maguire home. However, most significant of all is Kerry's performance. With twenty-four successes they are way ahead of the field — a reflection no doubt on the strength and supremacy of Kerry football.

The original 'Sam' was replaced in 1988. *Bhí a ré rithte.* It had taken many knocks in the tours of victory over six decades.

To the men of Meath goes the unusual dual honour of saying goodbye to the original 'Sam' and *Céad Míle Fáilte* to 'Sam Óg' as the new cup was initially dubbed.

Meath's superb 'Rock of Cashel', full-back Mick Lyons, was the last captain to receive the original 'Sam' after Meath's defeat of Cork in 1987 (their fourth title).

The following year, Meath centre forward, Joe Cassells — veteran of 100 battles over a period of fourteen years — proudly lifted the new cup.

A total of six captains have had the distinction of receiving the cup on two occasions, five of them in successive years: Joe Barrett, for Kerry in 1929 and 1932; Jimmy Murray, for Roscommon in 1943 and 1944; John Joe O'Reilly, for Cavan in 1947 and 1948; Sean Flanagan, for Mayo in 1950 and 1951; Enda Colleran, for Galway in 1965 and 1966; and Tony Hanahoe, for Dublin in 1976 and 1977.

Peadar Kearney, who wrote our National Anthem, knew Sam Maguire well and dedicated the following poem to his memory.

> *Proud to have hailed you friend,*
> *Long years ago!*
> *Amid the fogs and fumes of London Town,*
> *An Empire's mart —*
> *Astride the sluggish Thames,*
> *Building on plundered clans,*
> *Her dread renown!*
>
> *Strong in your deathless faith*
> *Oh heart of gold!*
> *Your kindly, generous smile*
> *Gave strength to all*
> *Who grasped your hand*
> *In that great brotherhood:*
> *Waiting throughout the years for Éire's call.*

Sam Maguire

THE NALLY STAND

The Nally Stand was built in 1952 and was located to the left of the Railway goal end of Croke Park. A small structure, its capacity was limited to 2,000 spectators. It was later linked up with the new Hogan Stand, the construction of which began five years later, in 1957.

The Stand was named after Pat Nally, a Fenian and member of the Supreme Council of the IRB. He was a native of Balla, County Mayo.

A Celtic cross, which cost £250, was erected to his memory in his home town in January 1900. The memorial was unveiled by Dr Mark Ryan, of London, who had preceded Pat as Connaught representative on the Supreme Council of the Irish Republican Brotherhood.

Pat Nally, like his fellow countyman Michael Davitt, was active in the Land War. The National Land League was to have a profound influence on the course of Irish history and, in 1879, Pat was instrumental in setting up the Mayo branch of the organisation.

According to Dr Donal McCartney, Dean of Arts at University College, Dublin, the Land League was: 'One of the most powerful democratic movements in all Irish history and its influence, both social and political, was profound.'

In the view of T.P. O'Neill, head of the Celtic Faculty at University College, Galway, 'The battles of Irish history, like Irish Songs, are sad. Few ended in victory. The Land League won not alone the battles but also the war.'

The organisation took its motto from the words of Young Irelander, James Fintan Lalor: 'the soil of Ireland for the people of Ireland'.

Pat Nally was a tall trim figure of a man and an athlete of note. In the province of Connaught, where he won countless trophies, he was without peer. His interest in Gaelic games,

P.W. Nally

however, appears to have been minimal; there is certainly no evidence that he ever played them. Athletics were his forte.

Pat was born in 1857, and christened Patrick William Nally. His father was a land owner and Pat was one of six sons. In keeping with the harsh economic times of those days, some of his brothers emigrated.

Pat was arrested in 1883 for alleged involvement in what was known as the Crossmolina Conspiracy case. At his trial he was convicted of treason, on rather flimsy evidence, and incarcerated in Mountjoy prison for a ten-year term.

At the time of the Parnell Commission (set up after an attempt was made to discredit Parnell), the authorities used bribery and promises of liberty in their attempts to get Nally to testify on behalf of *The Times*. He spurned their offers with contempt. He was well aware of the bribery, corruption and intimidation associated with the passing of the Act of Union in 1800. (A sum of £1.5 million had been paid in bribes, following which the Act was passed in the Irish Parliament by 158 to 115 votes.)

Good conduct saw his term of imprisonment reduced. However, he died while still in prison, on 9 November 1891, aged 34 — the day before he was to be released. The causes of his death remain a mystery to this day; officially it was stated that Pat Nally died from typhoid fever, but foul play was suspected.

Following a huge public funeral, he was buried in the Fenian plot in Glasnevin Cemetery. Mourners came from all over the country and there was a strong representation from the Dublin club which was named after him. Amongst those present as recorded by T. F. O'Sullivan were:

James Stephens; John O'Leary; P.N. Fitzgerald, Cork; John E. Redmond; Dr E. Kenny, MP; Jas O'Kelly, MP; John O'Connor, MP; John Clancy, MP; Edmund Leamy, MP; J. Harrington, MP; Pierce Mahony, MP (afterwards The O'Mahony, D.L.); Patrick O'Brien, MP; J.J. Dalton, MP; Michael Lambert; Dr Fitzgerald, MP; J.E. Kennedy, MP, TC;

John Clancy, TC, Sub-sheriff; J. Wyse Power, P. Hoctor, Limerick; J. Fitzgibbon, Castlerea; P.J. White, Clara; Anthony Mackey, Castleconnell; T. Ashe, TC, PLG, Galway; Patrick Tobin, Sec. GAA; F.J. Allen, J.W. O'Beirne; J.G. Judge; Joseph P. Quinn, Claremorris; Wm Kelly, President GAA, do; M. Killeen, T.B. Kelly, President Co. Mayo GAA.

Pat is believed to have had discussions, prior to his arrest, first with Maurice Davin, and later with Michael Cusack, on the development and promotion of athletics — an area of sport to which he was deeply committed.

The Nally Stand. Courtesy Mary Fullam

The (Original) Hogan Stand

The Hogan Stand was originally built in 1924 in preparation for the Tailteann games. It was located on the Jones's Road side of Croke Park, stretching from the sixty-yard mark to the twenty-one line at the Railway goal. It was officially opened in 1926 on St Patrick's Day. By present-day standards it was a modest construction, being a small wooden structure which sloped from ground level right up to roof level at the back. It had a seating capacity of 1,400 and those fortunate enough to get a seat had an excellent view of the game.

The stand was dedicated to the memory of Michael Hogan, the Tipperary footballer. He had been shot dead by a company of Black and Tans while a game of football, between Tipperary and Dublin, was in progress at Croke Park on 21 November 1920. That day has gone down in Irish history as Bloody Sunday.

In modern-day Irish the dedication plaque it would read as follows:

Gaeil Éireann
Do thiodhlaic an cábán so
I ndílchuimhne ar
Mhícheál Ó Hógáin ó Thiobraid Árann
agus ar
Thrí dhuine dhéag eile
do mhairbh Arm Shasana le feall annso
ar an nDomhnach dár dáta an 21 adh lá
de Shamhain 1920

The Stand was taken down after the Galway *v* Kerry National Football league final of 1956/57. It was removed to make way for the construction of a new Hogan Stand that would stretch the full length of the Jones's Road side of Croke Park. The old structure was re-located at Limerick Gaelic grounds. It remained there until the construction of the Mackey Stand — officially opened in 1988 — at which time it was demolished. It had served the public well for more than sixty years.

The last man to be presented with a trophy from the first Hogan Stand at Croke Park was Jack Mahon, Captain of the victorious Galway team in their clash with Kerry in the 1956/57 league final.

The old Hogan Stand

THE (SECOND) HOGAN STAND

Construction of the new Hogan Stand began in 1957 and, when completed, it replaced both the old Hogan Stand and the Long Stand.

The ten-year ticket system was introduced to facilitate its funding and (at the time of publication in 1999) a variation of this system is being used to help finance modern developments.

The official opening took place on 7 June 1959 and the ceremony was combined with the celebrations of the seventy-fifth Anniversary of the foundation of the GAA (1884).

The Railway Cup hurling final of that year, between Munster and Connaught, was postponed from St Patrick's Day to coincide with the official opening.

Munster won the match by 7:11 to 2:6, but unfortunately, the game wasn't one of the memorable ones associated with this competition. It was one of those days that Christy Ring ran riot and, at full forward, he scored 4:5. He would be 39 years of age the following October and was voted Texaco Hurler of the Year.

Michael Hogan after whom the original Hogan Stand was named

The new stand had a seating capacity of 16,000. It had a cantilevered upper deck and roof, and at the time was one of the finest and most modern of its type in Western Europe. It ran the full length of the Jones's Road side of the pitch.

Dr J.J. Stuart, the then President of the GAA, performed the opening ceremony and the attendance also included the President of Ireland, Seán T. O'Kelly, who made a speech.

On a historic day it was the performance of Ring, rather than the

Railway Cup final itself, that excited and left a lasting memory on the crowd of 23,248. The successful Munster team on that special occasion was as follows:

Mick Cashman(Cork)

Jimmy Brohan (Cork), Michael Maher (Tipperary)
John Barron (Waterford)

Tom McGarry (Limerick), Tony Wall (Tipperary),
Martin Óg Morrissey (Waterford)

Theo English (Tipperary), Tommy Casey (Limerick)

Donie Nealon (Tipperary), Seamus Power (Waterford),
Jimmy Doyle (Tipperary)

Jimmy Smyth (Clare), Christy Ring (Cork),
Larry Guinan (Waterford)

Subs: Jack Quaid (Limerick), Terry Kelly (Cork),
Richie McElligott (Kerry), Kieran Carey (Tipperary), Phil Grimes
(Waterford).

The current Hogan Stand will be demolished as the Croke Park Development Plan, currently in progress, proceeds through its various stages.

THE (OLD) CUSACK STAND

The original Cusack Stand was officially opened on Sunday, 21 August 1938, and a brass plate bore the following inscription:

Cusack Stand (1938)

Erected in memory of Michael Cusack, Founder and First Secretary of the GAA. Born on September 20th 1847 at Carron, Co. Clare and died at Dublin on November 27th 1906

The main event on the day that the stand was officially opened was the All-Ireland football semi-final between Laois and Kerry. A crowd of 31,160 spectators gathered to watch the game, which Kerry narrowly won by 2:6 to 2:4.

There were many household names on the Kerry team including the great Dan O'Keeffe, in goal; Paddy Kennedy (Captain, 1946); a prince of midfielders, Johnny Walsh; Bill Casey; Paddy Bawn Brosnan; Bill Dillon (Captain, 1941) and Sean Brosnan.

Laois had the Delaney clan — brothers Jack, Chris, Mick, Bill and their Uncle Tom; Tommy Murphy, 'The Boy Wonder' from Graiguecullen, and Danny Douglas, veteran of a 100 battles with club, county and province. Danny was born in 1906 and (at the time of going to press in 1999) is a hale and hearty 93-year-old. He still has a vivid recollection of all the colleagues and games of his sporting youth.

On the day of the semi-final, many considered Laois most unlucky not to have won. It was their third successive year as Leinster champions. In the 1936 All-Ireland semi-final they had beaten Cavan by 2:6 to 1:5, but lost heavily to Mayo in the final, on a day when everything went wrong for them. A year later in Cork, they drew with Kerry, 2:3 to 1:6. However, in the replay in Waterford, they lost by 1 point — 2:2 to 1:4 — and saw Kerry go on to beat Cavan in the final.

The contract for the Stand was signed with a Limerick building firm, McCaffrey & O'Carroll, in January 1936. Prior to the signing of the contract, and to facilitate the development, an exchange of small strips of land took place between the GAA and Belvedere College authorities. The Stand was built to a design by Nicholas O'Dwyer BE, and the on-site engineer was Denis Mitchell, who himself had won an All-Ireland football medal with Galway in 1934.

Work on the Cusack Stand finished eleven months behind schedule. The delay was caused by a strike of building workers which lasted from April to mid-October 1937. As a consequence, the hurling final of that year, between Tipperary and Kilkenny, was switched to Fitzgerald Stadium, Killarney. It had been opened on Whit Sunday 1936 and was dedicated to the memory of one of Kerry's greatest footballers, Dick Fitzgerald.

The 1937 final, between Kerry and Cavan, had been scheduled to be played at Croke Park on 26 September. As the building strike was still in progress, urgent negotiations took place between Padraig O'Caoimh, Secretary of the GAA, and the Building Trades Council. Following the discussions, agreement was reached and direct labour was allowed in to clear the site.

The Stand was declared officially open, on 21 August 1938, by the then GAA President, Padraig McNamee of Antrim

The old Cusack Stand

(the first President from the Northern Province), during half-time in the football semi-final. The construction had been a massive undertaking at the time and the original Cusack Stand served the GAA and its followers well, for over half a century.

The cost of the Stand was £52,000, a huge sum in those days. It was 407'3" long, 52'3" wide and, from ground to roof top, it measured 79' high. It accommodated 20,000 spectators in total — 5,000 seated in the upper deck and 15,000 standing below. In the mid-1960s seating for 9,000 was introduced to the lower deck, which, of course, reduced the overall capacity of the Stand.

Mícheál O'Hehir made his Croke Park broadcasting début on the day that the Cusack Stand was officially opened with a commentary on the Laois *v* Kerry game. He had made his début as a commentator at Mullingar, on 14 August 1938, for the All-Ireland football semi-final between Galway and Monaghan.

'Green Flag', writing in the *Irish Press* on the day prior to the opening, described the stand as 'a gem of engineering art'. However, the passage of time, which has the capacity to wither and decay most things, finally rendered the 'old' Cusack Stand obsolete. Its demolition began immediately after Derry recorded their first All-Ireland senior football win, with victory over Cork by 1:14 to 2:8, on 19 September 1993.

About eight hundred of the seats were taken to Austin Stack Park in Tralee to further enhance the excellent development there.

The 'old' Cusack Stand was replaced by the new Cusack Stand which was the first phase of the modernising Croke Park Development, a development that will make Croke Park compare very favourably with any stadium in the world.

THE (NEW) CUSACK STAND

Dreams sometimes undergo a metamorphosis and emerge into reality. So it was with the new Cusack Stand — the first phase of a development that would modernise Croke Park and proudly lead the GAA into the twenty-first century.

The dream took root, under the leadership of Director General Liam Mulvihill, during the Presidency of John Dowling of Offaly. It was further developed during the Presidencies of Peter Quinn (Fermanagh), Jack Boothman (Wicklow) and Joe McDonagh (Galway).

An immense amount of preparatory work went into the planning of the development programme. In an excellent article, in *The Irish Times* on 26 July 1995, Paddy Downey outlined the development details as follows:

> *When it was decided by the Central Council, more than six years ago, to replace the old Cusack and ultimately to rebuild the whole stadium, the GAA Director General, Liam Mulvihill, went to the British Sports Council for advice regarding the appointment of international experts in the field, who would draw up a master plan. Advice was forthcoming and eventually two Architectural companies which specialise in Sports Stadium design were appointed — H.O.K. (Helmut, Obata, Keesbaum) of Kansas City in the U.S. and an English group Howard Lobb & Partners.*
>
> *H.O.K's work throughout the U.S. includes the Giants Stadium in New Jersey, Arrowhead in Kansas City, Camden Yards in Baltimore, and Joe Robbie Stadium in Miami: Howard Lobb designed the only stand that is being retained in the new Twickenham and new stands at Goodwood, Ascot and Cheltenham.*
>
> *Appointed along with that team, to observe their work and consult, were the Irish Architectural firm, Gilroy McMahon, the GAA's own Consultant Engineers, Horgan and Lynch; Seamus Monahan & Partners, Quantity Surveyors, and J.V. Tierney & Co. Service Engineers.*
>
> *Meanwhile, GAA officials and representatives of the professionals visited more than thirty stadiums around the world, most of them in the U.S., the U.K., Germany, Spain, Italy and Holland.*
>
> *The international experts provided design directives in detail for a master plan but the physical design work finally fell into Gilroy*

McMahon's court. The original plan, when costed, was found to be too expensive — more than £50m — and, as well, it might have met insuperable problems with the Dublin Planning authorities.

The construction contract was signed with John Sisk and Sons Limited, on 25 August 1993, and demolition of the old Cusack Stand began the day after the All-Ireland senior football final of that year.

The new Cusack Stand was officially opened on Sunday, 3 September 1995, on All-Ireland senior hurling final day. It had seating capacity for just over 24,000 spectators. It was built at a cost of £40 million and it measures 484 feet in length and 110 feet 6 inches in height.

The project received finance from various sources. The corporate sector contributed roughly 50 per cent of the cost and acquired 15 per cent of the accommodation. Ten-year tickets (available only to GAA clubs, and not for general sale) admit the holder to All-Ireland football and hurling finals as well as any replays. For a fee of £5,000 Cusack Club Membership entitles members to a seat in the new stand, for all matches over a ten-year period, as well as a wide range of Club facilities. Membership is available to both individual GAA followers and the Irish business sector.

The cost of the entire new development will be in the region of £150 million and, when completed, the spectator capacity of Croke Park will be around 84,000 people.

The Artane Boys Band march past the new Cusack Stand
Courtesy Inpho Sports Photography

BLOODY SUNDAY

In 1920, a reign of terror stalked the land; it was to be a horrific year in Irish history. The Independence Movement was in full swing and guerrilla warfare was having an impact on the British authorities. In addition, Michael Collins had pierced the British Intelligence network and his spies were operating in Dublin Castle.

In March of that year the Black and Tans arrived in Ireland followed by the Auxiliaries, in August.

Piaras Béaslaí in his book, *Michael Collins and the Making of a New Ireland*, described the Black and Tans as

> *...a body whose unsavoury record stinks in the nostrils of the civilised world ... The origin of the name is not generally known. When the new English recruits to the RIC first made their appearance in Ireland, the usual RIC uniforms were not available for them, and they were dressed, for the time being, in khaki uniform with the black belts and caps of the RIC. Hence, the country people nicknamed them 'Black and Tans'. When the new force had distinguished themselves by many murders and outrages, and the sacking of towns, and the name had come to be a name of terror to peaceful citizens, they adopted it enthusiastically for themselves; and their special propagandist organ, issued from Dublin Castle, gloried in the term. At a later stage the term came to be applied, also popularly, to the Auxiliaries and English spies, and other agents of the Reign of Terror.*
>
> *The Black and Tans were largely drawn from criminal classes, and authentic cases were discovered where they had been released by a beneficent Government from penal servitude, incurred through revolting crimes, to enable them to bring the lights of English law and order to Ireland. They were, in short, dirty tools for a dirty job.*
>
> *Those of the old RIC who were left in the force viewed with disgust their compelled association with these off-scourings of rascaldom, who stole one another's money and belongings, who had no code of honour, no scruple, and very little discipline. But they were the right kind of men for Sir Hamar Greenwood's job.*

Of the Auxiliaries, Piaras Béaslaí had this to say:

They were stated officially to be composed exclusively of ex-officers of the British Army, but this, like most English official statements about Ireland, was untrue. A considerable proportion of them, but not all, were ex-officers; but the criminal element was also found amongst them. They were a very mixed body, containing some fine types, and a great many very low scoundrels.

This force was much more formidable than the ordinary Black and Tans owing to the superior intelligence, energy, and courage of its members. They became known as 'the Auxis'; and, in Dublin where the ordinary RIC did not operate they were commonly referred to as Black and Tans.

The whole country was in turmoil. Atrocities abounded and terror gripped the land. Conditions during that year resulted in a very reduced amount of GAA activities. Many young men were active in the Independence Movement, on the run, or in prison.

On 16 March 1920, Tomás MacCurtain, Lord Mayor of Cork, received a letter in the post. It bore a cross, beneath which were written the words:

Thomas MacCurtain prepare for death.
You are doomed.

Piaras Béaslaí reports as follows:

On 20th March at 1 a.m., a party of armed men, with blackened faces forced an entry into the house of Tomás MacCurtain, and shot him dead in the presence of his wife.... Public opinion in Cork was shown by the Coroner's jury, which after an enquiry lasting sixteen days, returned the following verdict:

We find that Alderman Tomás MacCurtain, Lord Mayor of Cork, died from shock and haemorrhage, caused by bullet wounds, and that he was wilfully wounded under circumstances of the most callous brutality; and that the murder was organised and carried out by the RIC officially directed by the British Government.

We return a verdict of wilful murder against David Lloyd George, Prime Minister of England; Lord French, Lord Lieutenant of Ireland; Ian MacPherson, late Chief Secretary of Ireland; acting-inspector General Smith, of the RIC; Divisional Inspector Clayton of the RIC; D.I. Swanzy, and some unknown members of the RIC.

He was succeeded as Lord Mayor by Terence McSwiney whose inaugural address contained the following:

This contest is one of endurance, and it is not they who can inflict most, but they who can suffer most, who will conquer.

Some of those in the Movement used the hunger strike as a weapon — as did Terence McSwiney during his imprisonment in Brixton Prison.

After a fast of seventy four days Terence McSwiney died, on Oct. 25th ... the event caused intense emotion throughout Ireland, and, indeed, among the Irish race all over the world. The body of the martyred Mayor of Cork was brought to Holyhead for the purpose of embarking it for Dublin. Here a disgraceful scene took place. A body of Auxiliaries seized the coffin from the relatives, and put it on board a boat, which conveyed it to Cork.

And so the struggle continued in every shape and form, with the 'Tans' terrorising the civilian population.

Piaras Béaslaí further records the following:

On the morning of Nov. 21st parties of volunteers raided houses in various parts of Dublin and fourteen English officers were shot dead ... as a 'reprisal' the Auxiliaries rode up in lorries to Croke Park that afternoon, where a huge crowd of men, women and children were engaged in watching a Gaelic football match between Dublin and Tipperary, and fired on the crowd killing 14, and wounding about 60. One of the players in the match was among the killed. They then dismounted and searched all the men in the Park. By way of justification it was alleged that they were fired on — a statement palpably absurd. It was also alleged that they had information that the shootings that morning had been done by men from the country who had come up for that purpose, under guise of attending a match, and that this was the reason for the raid on Croke Park ... all the men engaged on the operation that morning belonged to 'The Squad' or the Dublin Brigade.

A Group of Dublin Black and Tans (Auxiliaries)

Pádraig Puirséal in his excellent book *The GAA in its Time* gave the following account:

> *An inter-county football challenge between Tipperary and Dublin was fixed for Croke Park on Sunday 21st Nov. On that morning a number of British Secret Service Agents, known as the 'Cairo Gang' were shot in their bedrooms. As reprisals were expected, GAA officials met at Croke Park to consider calling off the match, but decided to go ahead with it. The game was not long in progress when two lorry loads of Black and Tans arrived and fired volley after volley into the crowd which numbered about 10,000.*

In the words of Phil O'Neill (Sliabh Ruadh), 'The scene was indescribable as the thousands present sought every means to escape from the deadly fusillade. The pleasant picture was changed into a bloody pandemonium'.

Members of Michael Collins' Counter-Intelligence Service, known as The Apostles

The infamous Cairo Gang

In an article in the *Sunday Tribune*, Denis Walsh painted a graphic account of the events of the day as the following excerpts show.

About ten thousand people turned up in Croke Park that afternoon. Shortly after 2.45 p.m. Mick Sammon of Kildare threw the ball in. The first half wasn't long on when an aeroplane flew over the pitch and a red flare was shot from the cockpit.

Shortly afterwards, Black and Tans appeared on one of the walls around the ground and an officer on top of the wall fired a revolver shot. It was the signal for the first volley of gunfire.

At first it was thought that they were firing blanks, but that theory was quickly disabused. Machine gunfire rang out in increasing volume. Some of it clattered into the corrugated iron roofing on the dressing-rooms, where a part of the crowd had positioned itself, adding to the racket.

The crowd stampeded towards the wall furthest from the gunfire in an attempt to scramble free. On the pitch, the players dispersed and joined the rush. All the players except two: Mick Hogan and Jim Egan of Tipperary. They lay on the ground, one on the grass, one on the cinder track that surrounded the field.

Egan eventually got to his feet, covered in Hogan's blood, and walked towards a priest in the crowd. By this time, the soldiers had corralled the thousands who hadn't made good their escape and had herded the Tipperary players in a separate group.

Father Crotty came over to administer Last Rites. A man called Thomas Ryan had whispered an Act of Contrition in Hogan's ear, but was shot dead while he knelt by Hogan's side. Hogan had been hit in the head and under the left shoulder and was dead before the priest arrived.

The crowd was searched while the Tipperary players waited, expecting to be killed. Tommy Ryan was the only Tipperary player who managed to get outside the ground, but the Black and Tans discovered him in a house in Clonliffe Road.

Two of the Black and Tans were about to shoot him when an officer walked in and stopped them. 'I don't think he acted from motives of mercy', says Ryan. 'He just wanted to be tidy and, instead of having odd shootings here and there, he wanted them all done together in Croke Park.'

Ryan wore a tricolour on his shorts and socks, so they ripped his gear off with their bayonets and walked him, naked, back to the pitch. As he walked along, a man took off his coat and gave it to him; for his charity he got a blow with the butt of a rifle.

The Black and Tans drove off, trailing the tricolour that was always flown at Croke Park from the back of the lorry. No official enquiry was ever held, but horror at the incident was expressed abroad as well as at home ....

On the morning after the match, Tipperary Captain Ned O'Shea wired news of the shooting to Grangemockler. Two local priests brought the news to Hogan's mother ....

Mick's remains were removed from Jervis Street Hospital to the pro-Cathedral on Tuesday. On Wednesday, they were transported by train to Clonmel and a glass lid was fitted to the coffin. They dressed the corpse in Jack Kickham's football jersey and, on Thursday, he was buried ....

In 1927, a white marble monument was erected to Hogan at the family plot in Grangemockler Cemetery ....

Years after the shooting, a high-ranking officer in the Auxiliaries revealed that on the day, they couldn't decide whether to burn and loot O'Connell St. or raid the football match. So they tossed a coin.

They tossed a coin.

THE JIMMY COONEY CASE AND 'THE BAN' — 1938

In many respects, probably the most celebrated case concerning 'the Ban' (Rule 27), in the history of the GAA, is that of Jimmy Cooney.

In brief, Rule 27 had stipulated that, attendance at, involvement in, or promotion of foreign games, that is, rugby, soccer, cricket and hockey, rendered one liable to a suspension, the term of which could vary depending on the nature of the offence.

In a thrilling Munster final in 1937, Tipperary had defeated Limerick. They then went on to a somewhat facile win over Kilkenny in the All-Ireland final which was played at Fitzgerald Stadium, Killarney. Tipperary seemed to be a formidable team and looked set to make it two in a row in 1938. However, the Cooney case blighted and eventually killed their prospects.

In those days, if a player resided outside his native county he had to indicate his intention of playing with his county by signing a Declaration form before a certain date each year.

Jimmy Cooney, a native of Carrick-on-Suir, was resident in Dublin and played with UCD. On 2 February 1938, he completed his Declaration form and forwarded it to the Tipperary County Board. For some reason it wasn't sent onwards to the General Secretary of the GAA until shortly before Easter and therein lay the basis of future conflict. (Note the timing of these two events.)

On 12 February 1938, Jimmy attended an international rugby match in Dublin. He was reported to the GAA authorities, probably by the Vigilance Committee. He admitted the offence and accordingly incurred an automatic suspension of three months.

In due course, he applied for re-instatement and this was granted by the Leinster Council with effect from 14 May 1938. Thus, on the face of it, everything appeared to be in order for

Jimmy to play with Tipperary in the championship — but there is many a slip....

Now, back in the fold — or so he thought — Jimmy played for Tipperary in a Monaghan Cup game in London against Limerick. This proved to be the match that sparked off the controversy. The Central Council of the GAA held that although Jimmy's Declaration was dated February 1938, it was effective only from the date of receipt by them — Eastertime 1938. Further, in the Council's view, the Declaration was deemed to have been made by Jimmy during the period of his suspension and was therefore invalid.

Accordingly, he was declared illegal for the Monaghan Cup game and an automatic suspension of six months followed. There was fury in Tipperary and the County Board held that the effective date of the Declaration was 2 February. Not so, said the Central Council, insisting that the effective date was when the document came into their possession just before Easter. In order to clarify the matter and ensure that there would be no further misunderstanding, the Tipperary County Board was officially informed, by Central Council, that Jimmy Cooney was a suspended player. The notification came on the eve of their Munster semi-final game with Clare.

In Tipperary, feelings were running high about the matter. Yet there was a school of thought that counselled against playing Jimmy. However, any such advice was disregarded.

Tipperary lined out against Clare in the Munster semi-final, at Limerick on 26 June, with Jimmy Cooney at midfield. It caused quite a stir among the spectators who were in no doubt about the consequences. Clare indicated that they would lodge an objection if they lost the game.

Lose it they did, as Tipperary demonstrated their superiority with a 3:10 to 2:3 victory. They would have won without Jimmy Cooney.

Clare's objection was upheld by the Munster Council. There followed a counter objection from Tipperary to the effect that Michael Griffin, a member of the Clare team, had also attended the rugby match that Jimmy Cooney had been seen at. The source of this evidence was Cooney. Coming from a suspended player, the evidence was ruled as inadmissible.

However, Tipperary were not prepared to let the matter rest at that. They appealed to the Central Council but lost their case. For Jimmy Cooney, it meant a suspension of six months and, in Tipperary, the matter caused a considerable amount of discontent as many pondered the probability that an All-Ireland title had been let slip.

In the course of writing my book, *Giants of the Ash*, I met with John Maher, one of Tipperary's great centre backs and we talked about the case. He recalled John Joe Sheehy of Kerry saying to him that once Jimmy Cooney admitted being at the match the case became open and shut. Denial would have placed the onus of proof on the GAA and that might have proven difficult for the Association. However, there was also another side to this story. It was believed in some quarters that Jimmy was an opponent of 'the Ban' — he couldn't see the logic of not being able to attend a game, whatever about playing it. In attending the game it was believed he was attempting a crusade against 'the Ban'. This would not have gone down well at GAA Headquarters and could well explain their stand on what constituted the effective date of the Declaration form.

Jimmy Cooney and his wife, Angela, at their wedding in 1942
Courtesy Seamus Cooney

When I was writing *Legends of the Ash*, Tom McInerney of Clare mentioned the Jimmy Cooney incident to me. He remembered Canon Hamilton of Clare pleading with Johnny Leahy not to play Cooney. Clare didn't like the idea of objecting but, according to Tom, they were under specific instructions from the Leinster Council to do so. Johnny Leahy, who at that late stage was hardly in a position to alter the Tipperary stance, simply replied, 'We'll talk about that after the match.'

From the inception of the GAA, 'the Ban' was quite an emotive issue. The following is a little of its early history as per *The Gaelic Athletic Annual 1934/5*:

- 27 September 1886 at a Meeting in Thurles: Players of non-Gaelic games barred
- 4 January 1888 at Congress in Thurles: Police barred from membership
- 16 April 1893 at Congress in Thurles: Rule banning police rescinded
- 22 September 1901 at Congress in Thurles: Resolution against imported games passed
- 30 November 1902 at Congress in Thurles: Ban on foreign games made compulsory
- 11 January 1903 at an adjourned Congress in Thurles: British Armed Forces debarred
- 13 December 1903 at Congress in Thurles: Ban on foreign games made optional with counties
- 8 January 1905 at Congress in Thurles: Ban on foreign games re-enacted

'The Ban' and its existence meant different things to different people. For example, take the case of Mick Darcy, as told to me by Kilkenny man John Dowling, a teacher in Good Counsel College, New Ross. John himself had had many hurling successes in his UCD days — two Fitzgibbon Cup medals, a Dublin county league title, runner-up in a county final against Young Irelands. He had known Mick well during these times.

Mick, a great Tipperary hurler of the 1920s, was Chairman of the UCD hurling and football club. He loved our Gaelic games, particularly hurling, and he encouraged everyone to play them. After a game he would say to the players, 'You were great, you were great, well done', even though you might have played rather poorly — just seeing people play was a source of deep satisfaction to Mick. The Fitzgibbon Cup victories over arch-rivals UCC gave him immense pleasure. The rivalry was healthy but ferociously intense.

All who came in touch with Mick loved him for his integrity and dedication and gentlemanliness.

Then one day in the 1960s, the students decided to draft a motion for the removal of 'the Ban'. Mick was distressed and he explained his position. He recalled for the students the day when he was spat on by a member of the Crown Forces as he entered Croke Park. For him, it was the ultimate humiliation and the memory was never erased. The scar on his mind reflected a deep wound. With sadness, he told the students he would have to resign as Chairman if they proceeded with the motion. Students can be radical and idealistic, but so deep was the esteem and affection in which they held Mick that they withdrew the motion.

Discussion of 'the Ban' could generate intense feelings and much heated argument. For several decades, whenever it came up at Congress, history, idealism and national feeling would be expounded upon by very eloquent, sincere and well-meaning delegates. This always resulted in motions for its abolition or investigation, being heavily defeated.

On 11 July 1921, a truce was called in the War of Independence. This ultimately resulted in the Anglo-Irish Treaty of 6 December 1921. After ratification of the Treaty, in the Dáil — by 64 votes to 57 — on Saturday, 7 January 1922, a twenty-six-county Free State was established. This might well have caused many to take the view that the days of 'the Ban' had served their purpose and should end.

So for three successive years — 1923, 1924 and 1925 — motions came before Congress to abolish it. All failed. In 1926, Congress — probably weary of the annual debate — decided that thereafter, 'the Ban' could be discussed only every three years. The years rolled on but the subject never really died.

There was further controversy, in 1938, when Dr Douglas Hyde, President of Ireland and a founder of Conradh na Gaeilge, was removed by the GAA authorities from his position as Patron. The decision was made because Dr Hyde had attended an international soccer match in his capacity as President of Ireland. There was a sense of outrage, both within and without GAA circles, over the Association's decision to remove him. To have treated a man of his stature this way, in his ageing years — a man who had worked unceasingly all his life for the promotion of all things Gaelic — hurt many people very deeply. He was never re-instated but his memory is perpetuated in Roscommon where the GAA County Grounds are named Dr Hyde Park as a tribute to him.

In the 1960s, when motions to remove 'the Ban' failed heavily at the Congresses of 1962, 1965 and 1968, there was no indication that its end was in sight. However, at the 1968 Congress, a Mayo motion was approved to set up a special committee to examine 'the Ban', in the context of the present day, and its findings were issued in November 1970.

At the Congress of 1971, held at Queen's University, Belfast, the representatives of thirty of the thirty-two counties voted for its removal and Congress approved. Also removed was the Ban on 'foreign dancing' — Rule 29.

Down through the decades some counties paid little attention to 'the Ban'. Others, however, were zealous in its implementation. Many players ignored it and played whatever combination of games they were proficient at and enjoyed. For them, a game was a game. As far as they were concerned, games were to be played and enjoyed or watched and relished and were

Douglas Hyde

sources of fulfilment and satisfaction, of friendship and comradeship — always provided, of course, that they were never caught at any 'banned' activity.

However, not all such players were lucky enough to escape detection. Sean Herbert of Limerick was suspended and it cost him an All-Ireland minor medal in 1940. Years later, fellow countyman Tom McGarry fell foul of the Association for playing soccer. Dave Creedon, of Cork, became persona non grata in 1937 for the same reason, and it cost him an All-Ireland minor hurling medal.

Then there was Tom Cheasty of Waterford who went to a soccer dance, was subsequently suspended, and consequently missed the National league final of 1963 and the winner's medal that went with it. Willie Barron, also of Waterford, went for 'a kind of a soccer trial kickabout' and was banished for two years for his alien activities. There were many others who were suspended, including Jack Lynch and Seannie Carroll of Cork. However, a case against 'Wilkie' Thorpe of Wexford failed for lack of conclusive evidence.

It is said that Mick Mackey used to go to rugby and soccer matches and so, to keep him from being suspended, he was put on the Vigilance committee. He was, however, never known to have reported anyone.

Jimmy Cooney was probably at his hurling peak in 1938; he was a brilliant hurler and outstanding midfielder. The controversy saw his career go into decline, and when he played with Limerick in the early 1940s, he was no longer the superb hurler of his earlier days.

After a meeting with Jimmy's son, Seamus, I have been able to take a closer look at the man himself. Jimmy was '...an all round sportsman who reached high levels of proficiency at football, hurling, handball and golf — a man who put the affair of 1938 behind him, rarely referred to it, but never lost his love for the game.'

Jimmy was born in 1914 and grew up in Carrick-on-Suir where he was associated with the Carrick Davins Club. His first sporting love was football and he was sufficiently talented to play at minor and junior level for Tipperary

However, the arrival, to Carrick-on-Suir CBS of Brother Madden, from Galway, changed the order of sporting priorities, and Jimmy was 'converted' to hurling — as indeed were many others. He climbed to the top quickly. In 1932, he won All-Ireland minor honours with his native Tipperary team. A junior All-Ireland triumph followed for Jimmy in 1933, and by 1934, he had progressed to the senior panel. Three years later, in 1937, a decisive victory over Kilkenny at Killarney completed a triple crown of titles for Jimmy. He was 23 and had tasted success at county level in all categories.

Earlier that year, on St Patrick's Day, Jimmy reached the pinnacle of the hurling world. On this occasion he played at centre field on the Munster Railway cup team that defeated Leinster by 1:9 to 3:1. He was in the company of greats and to be there was a reflection of his status. The Munster team — a host of hurling giants — was as follows:

Paddy Scanlon (Limerick)

John Maher (Tipperary), Tom McCarthy (Limerick)
Mick Kennedy (Limerick)

John Keane (Waterford), Paddy Clohessy (Limerick)
Larry Blake (Clare)

Timmy Ryan (Limerick), Jimmy Cooney (Tipperary)

John Mackey (Limerick), Mick Mackey (Limerick)
Christy Moylan (Waterford)

Micka Brennan (Cork), Paddy McMahon (Limerick)
Johnny Quirke (Cork)

In 1936, Jimmy played as a sub on the Munster team that was beaten by Leinster by 1 point in the final. Then in 1938, he was again selected for Munster but the suspension ruled him out.

Having completed his secondary education he studied engineering at UCD and qualified with a BE degree in 1937. He joined the ESB and went from there to the army.

In his time, he played with several well-known clubs including Ahane, Blackrock, UCD (with whom he won a Dublin senior championship hurling title) and Tarbert in the Kerry senior championship.

He attended the rugby match at Lansdowne Road in 1938 in the company of his sweetheart and wife to be Angela Egan — they married in 1942. Angela won All-Ireland senior camogie titles with Dublin in 1937 and 1938. It must surely be a unique husband-and-wife record for both to have won senior All-Ireland honours in hurling and camogie in the same year.

Following an interview with John D. Hickey, an article appeared in the *Irish Independent*, on 8 January 1965, from which the following is an extract:

The '64 Tipp. team played the best hurling he ever saw in the 1963/64 National league final against Wexford. Others may see a forward line as good as the six that played for Tipp. that day but I know that I will never again see anything like it.

I don't care what anyone says about other players but Mick Mackey was undoubtedly the best-ever hurler.

His views on midfielders of his time. There was of course what might be termed the Tipp. triumvirate in Dublin in those days — Tommy Treacy, Ned Wade, Mick Daniels — Harry Gray (Laois and Dublin) Timmy Ryan (Limerick). That's about the lot.

The best all round and most consistent team ever was the Limerick side of the thirties and the most versatile player of all was Jackie Power of that team. You would play him anywhere from right full back to left full forward and he would star. He was a wonderful player by any standards.

I regard the drawn Waterford/Kilkenny All-Ireland in 1959 as the best match I ever saw. It was wonderful hurling.

The matches that stand out most in his memory are the 1937 Munster final in which Tipp. made the breakthrough against a great Limerick team, and the massacre of the Mardyke, a Fitzgibbon Cup final in which UCC defeated UCD. In that University decider, the only one of five in which Jimmy was on the losing side, three UCD players, including the army man were carried off.

A natural athlete, he won on four successive occasions, the All-army golf championship, and at his best played off a three handicap.

In 1942 the seventh Brigade team, of which he and Mick Mackey were members, took the All-army hurling championship.

Jimmy served in the Congo in 1961/62 as Adjutant to Lieutenant General Sean MacEoin, former Chief of Staff and Supreme Commander of the UN forces (a body of 20,000 troops from many nations).

He was Director General of Engineering in the army with the rank of Colonel when his untimely death occurred in 1975. He was 61 years old. Four years earlier in 1971, he had seen 'the ban', which he so disliked, abolished.

A hurling colleague, in the course of an Appreciation after his death, had this to say:

He was a lad who had an intense love for the game of the Gael and never played any other. Injustice he could not abide and the effect of seeing across from him at the half way line in Limerick's Gaelic grounds on the day Tipperary 'defied' the ruling authority, a player who was with him at the 'debarred' game, was profound....

To his army duties he brought the same dedication and intensity of purpose, and his brilliant mathematical mind brought for him the rapid distinctions that put him in charge of engineering....

I bPairc Imeartha na bhFlaitheas go gcastar sinn aris a Shéamais.

Jimmy Cooney on UN service in the Congo 1961/62
Courtesy Seamus Cooney

THE JIMMY COONEY CASE
AND LOST TIME — 1998

According to Einstein's Theory of Relativity, time is a fourth dimension.

Well, time, or the absence of it, certainly added an extra dimension to the All-Ireland senior hurling semi-final replay of 1998. Clare and Offaly were the contenders in this contest which was played at Croke Park on Saturday 22 August that year.

It all happened when referee Jimmy Cooney, of Galway, blew full-time with two minutes of normal time remaining. Added-on time, or injury time, is at the discretion of the referee. As the 'extra' time in this match probably amounted to three minutes, anything from two to five minutes remained to be played when the final whistle blew. The score stood at Clare 1:16 (19); Offaly 2:10 (16).

When the whistle blew, Clare, in possession of the sliotar, were attacking close to the Offaly goal. Offaly, who had been down by ten points at one stage in the second half, were on a rampant recovery curve — but only the gods now know what drama, excitement and heroics were destined for those closing moments.

Jimmy had made a time-keeping error. He believed, at the time he blew the whistle, that the three minutes' injury time had actually played. It seems he had mixed up a thirty-five minute half with a thirty-minute half. In his report, he stated that he '...had erred in terminating the game'. It had been a game brimful of all that is great and majestic in the ancient craft of hurling. A game, as journalist Kevin Cashman wrote, of '...hurling as we maligned traditionalists know and love it: hard, direct, replete with good ground strokes and magnificent lift and strike'.

With Jimmy Cooney in mind, I decided to look up what M. Scott Peck had written for 22 August, in his book, *Meditations from the Road*. The entry for that day is as follows: 'It is not impractical to consider seriously changing the rules of the game when the game is clearly killing you.' Strangely prophetic words!

The time-keeping error presented the GAA authorities with a situation they hadn't faced before, certainly not at that level of the championship.

The solution was found in the Rule Book. On Sunday, 23 August 1998, a specially-convened meeting of the Games Administration Committee discussed the issue. Following this meeting the Committee released a statement which said that, in accordance with Rule 138 of the official guide, they had no option but to re-fix the game.

Rule 138 states that should players, officials or supporters be found responsible for terminating a match, then the team in question is liable to disqualification, but that if a match 'is prematurely ended for any other reason, it shall be re-fixed for the full period'.

The prologue to the affair was the exciting game of 9 August 1998 in which the two teams had drawn, scoring 1:13 each. In this match Clare had had to line out without Brian Lohan and Colin Lynch who had been suspended. It was a game where Offaly's never-say-die spirit almost carried the day.

The sequel took place Thurles on 29 August 1998. It is interesting to take a look at the different paths that Clare and Offaly had taken to reach this game.

Clare's Passage

Clare 0:21; Cork 0:13 — 21 June
    at Semple Stadium, Thurles

Clare 1:16; Waterford 3:10 — 12 July
    at Semple Stadium, Thurles

Clare 2:16; Waterford 0:10 — 19 July
    at Semple Stadium, Thurles

Clare 1:13; Offaly 1:13 — 9 August at Croke Park

Clare 1:16; Offaly 2:10 — 22 August at Croke Park

Clare Team — 1998

Offaly Team — 1998

Offaly's Journey

Offaly 4:28; Meath 0:8 — 24 May at Croke Park

Offaly 1:15; Wexford 0:17 — 14 June at Croke Park

Offaly 1:11; Kilkenny 3:10 — 5 July at Croke Park

Offaly 2:18; Antrim 2:9 — 26 July at Croke Park

Offaly 1:13; Clare 1:13 — 9 August at Croke Park

Offaly 2:10; Clare 1:16 — 22 August at Croke Park

Ebbing and flowing, the outcome of the replay hung in the balance all the way — and never more tantalisingly than in the closing minutes. With the score at Offaly 0:16; Clare 0:10, Clare cut the deficit to three points with three scores and their every onslaught sought an equalising goal. But in vain. The Offaly defence, and magnificent goalkeeping by Stephen Byrne, held the fort superbly.

The opening half was breathtaking — the hurling glorious and the pace furious — it was hurling in all its stern, naked grandeur.

Over the entire seventy minutes of play, Offaly were crisp, assured and direct. Possession was well used and energy was well conserved. Joe Dooley, father of the field, had five glorious points from play — distance and angles mattered not — and thereby hangs a tale.

At the call of time, before an attendance of over 42,000, the scoreboard read Offaly 0:16; Clare 0:13. It had been a spellbinding encounter.

Offaly then turned their minds to the second Sunday in September when they would face Kilkenny in the All-Ireland final. It would be their eighth game of the championship — five wins and two losses up to then. Now, they had all to play for with one last throw of the dice.

Clare set forth to cross the Shannon — the long Odyssey of a turbulent summer now ended. So much of their hurling had been vintage stuff. Now, on the way home — and for quite a while to come — they must surely dwell on 'the slings and arrows of outrageous fortune'.

THE WALK-OVER FINAL OF 1911

In the early years of GAA competition, championships did not reach the final stage an on annual basis for a variety of reasons. Indeed, there were occasions when finals were played almost two years later than the year of their championship.

In this regard, the 1911 All-Ireland hurling championship didn't fair too badly. Its final was scheduled for 18 February 1912, at Cork Athletic Grounds. The finalists were Limerick and Kilkenny and an epic contest was in prospect. Limerick were a rising force led by the stout-hearted John 'Tyler' Mackey, while Kilkenny were an established power and famed throughout the land.

It was Limerick's second appearance in a final with Kilkenny. In 1897, with a Kilfinane selection, they had defeated Kilkenny, with a Tullaroan selection, by 3:4 to 2:4, and captured their first title.

In the 1911 championship, Kilkenny were contesting their ninth final and hoping to add to the four titles that they had won since their first in 1904.

To qualify for the final, Limerick had beaten Kerry in the first round, at Listowel, by 6:5 to 1:2. This was followed by a convincing win over Clare, in Tipperary, by 10:5 to 6:1. Meanwhile, Tipperary had caused quite a shock by defeating Cork, by 5:2 to 0:3, in Dungarvan. The scene was now set for a Munster final between Limerick and Tipperary. Followers looked forward to a stirring encounter between these two powerful teams — Tipperary, the defeated All-Ireland finalists of 1909, and Limerick, the defeated All-Ireland finalists of 1910. Both teams believed they could go the full distance in 1911.

The final was played on 19 November, at Cork Athletic Grounds, before a crowd of 6,000 spectators who certainly got value for money. The score was level at half-time with the teams on 1:2 each. In a thrilling finish Limerick put in a final ten-minute rally to come from 7 points down and steal victory by a goal. The final score was: Limerick 5:3; Tipperary 4:3. It was a famous victory — made more famous still by virtue of the fact that it was over the legendary Tipperary 'Thurles Blues'. The 'Blues' selection boasted great names like Hugh Shelly the Captain, 'Hawk' O'Brien in goal, Paddy Brolan, Bob Mockler, Andy Carew, Tom Gleeson and Johnny Leahy.

It seems unreal nowadays to think of an All-Ireland semi-final being played on 31 December. But that's the way it was on New Year's Eve 1911 when Limerick met and defeated Galway, at Portlaoise, by 7:4 to 2:6.

This is how Tom Ryall in his book, *Kilkenny The GAA Story 1884–1984*, described Kilkenny's path to the final:

> *Wexford were the reigning All-Ireland champions when they met Kilkenny in Dungarvan in the Leinster semi-final of the 1911 championship. The game was originally fixed for Waterford, but Wexford objected, claiming it was not a neutral ground as it was only four miles from Mooncoin. The match lived up to the highest expectations. Kilkenny led at half-time by 3:3 to 1:1. Wexford made it hard to get scores in the second half and at full time Kilkenny had won by 4:4 to 1:1. The winners' goal in the closing half, scored by Jimmy Kelly, only came in the closing minutes.*
>
> *Kilkenny avenged their defeat of the previous year by Dublin, in the Leinster final. This was played in Portlaoise. It took Kilkenny a long time to get into their stride. Dick Grace played well but was reported 'to be still putting his hand to the man', resulting in conceding frees. Tom McCormack, Sim Walton, 'Drug' Walsh and Jack Rochford were the best players. Kilkenny led by 2:2 to 2 goals at half-time. They improved in the second half to run out winners by 4:6 to 3:1. Then they had to fight hard to win against Antrim in the All-Ireland semi-final which was played at Jones's Road, now Croke Park. Kilkenny won by 5:5 to 1:1 after leading at half-time by 1:4 to a goal.*
>
> *The All-Ireland final was against Limerick and was fixed for the Cork Athletic grounds. Prior to the game, John F. Drennan of Conway Hall presented a set of black and amber jerseys to the Kilkenny County Board to be worn by the County team. Thereafter, these were the colours worn by Kilkenny.*

It is worth taking time to digress briefly and record a unique piece of Kilkenny GAA history. On 22 October 1911, at Jones's Road, Kilkenny defeated Meath in the Leinster senior football final by 2:4 to 1:1. That victory made it a Kilkenny double in

Leinster. 'Sliabh Ruadh', in his *History of the GAA 1910–1930*,
said, 'Meath, who had beaten Dublin, were fancied to pull off
the issue, but the sturdy men from Knocktopher and the Quarry
played clever, robust football and emerged victors'.

The football men who made history for Kilkenny on the day
were: Dick Holohan — Captain, Dick Dalton, Jim Dwyer,
W. Dalton, Pat Power, Tom Brennan (Knocktopher), J.
Donovan, 'A.N. Other', Jim Coady, Jim Hoyne, Paddy
O'Neill, Willie Hoynes (Miners), J. Saunders, J. Fitzgerald,
(Coolagh). The game was refereed by M.F. Crowe, of Dublin.

History aside, however, a record crowd was expected for the
1911 championship final and both teams had household names
in their line-up. Playing for Kilkenny were: Sim Walton, John
T. Power, Dan Kennedy, The Graces, The Doyles, Matt Gargan
and Jack Rochford. In the Limerick line-out were: Egan Clancy,
Jack Ryan in goal, Mick Harrington, Ned Treacy, Mick Feely,
Stephen Gleeson, led by the redoubtable John 'Tyler' Mackey.

Heavy rain marred the occasion, for which over 12,000
spectators had assembled. An inspection of the pitch, by the
referee, Tom Kenny of Galway, and Central Council officials,
resulted in the game's being called off. However, the Limerick
team had appeared on the pitch and had done a bit of limbering
up and pucking about. Previously, they had played Tipperary at
the same venue, in what they considered similar conditions, and
were convinced the game should go ahead; but their efforts to
influence the decision were all to no avail.

There is no evidence to suggest that Kilkenny weren't
prepared to play. Limerick went through the ritual of claiming
the match, chairing 'Tyler' Mackey off the pitch and declaring
themselves All-Ireland champions. All of that, however, was
really just make-believe.

The match, with Tom Irwin of Cork as referee, was fixed for
Thurles on 21 April and therein lay the kernel of the trouble
that lay ahead — Limerick dug in and said, 'Cork or nowhere'.

The late Sean Herbert told me the thinking behind
Limerick's decision to insist on a Cork venue. It appears, that
after Limerick's defeat of Tipperary in the Munster final, in
Cork, Tipperary made an objection against them but the
objection was not upheld. This led 'Tyler' Mackey, who could

be strong-headed and impetuous on occasion, to hold the opinion that Thurles could not be viewed as a neutral venue. Limerick refused to travel and tabled a motion for Congress to change the venue but the motion was heavily defeated. The game was again re-fixed for Thurles — this time for 18 May 1911 — but the word from Limerick was still the same: 'Cork or nowhere'. It had become a matter of principle for Limerick, which, when objectively viewed, was suicidal to adhere to.

On 2 June the Central Council took decisive action and Kilkenny were awarded the All-Ireland title. However, in so doing, the Central Council realised it was going to suffer a considerable loss of revenue at a time when they were struggling financially. As a follow-up, the Limerick County Board was suspended. (Without a county board, and until it was reinstated, in 1912, Limerick could not participate in the championships.)

In an attempt to recoup some of the lost revenue a match was arranged between Kilkenny and Munster finalists, Tipperary, to be played in Dungarvan. A special set of medals was made for the occasion. Kilkenny won on the score of 3:3 to 2:1 and the game was refereed by Harry Boland.

Thus ended a most unfortunate saga in the history of the GAA. It was the only occasion when a walk-over was awarded in a senior hurling final. Viewed from today's standpoint the whole débâcle seems incomprehensible. Tact and diplomacy, negotiation and communication all appear to have failed in 1911.

No one is alive now to tell us, firsthand, exactly how unsuitable the ground was for play in 1911. To this day, there are people who wonder whether the conditions were any worse than in 1935 when Limerick and Kilkenny played an All-Ireland thriller; or in 1939, when Cork and Kilkenny served up epic play in thunder and lightning and rain; or in the early 1950s, when Clare and Wexford produced a most memorable Oireachtas hurling final on a sodden rain-soaked pitch. In more recent times, those who were privileged to be present at the Leinster final of 1995 will never forget the classic play served up by Offaly and Kilkenny, despite thunder, lightning and torrential rain. It was squelch, squelch, as the players ran to contest the sliotar; and when they whipped on the ground ball, the surface water whizzed along the sliotar's path.

Atrocious weather at Croke Park at the 1935 Final. Courtesy *Irish Independent*

The following is a fascinating excerpt from an article by Gertrude Gaffney in the *Irish Independent* on Monday, 2 September 1935 (it appeared following the All-Ireland final of that year, between Kilkenny and Limerick, and was entitled, 'The Scenes in the Rain'):

It was just a chance that I saw the hurling final because five minutes or so after I got into Croke Park I started out of it again and but for the valour of a friend I would have been at home instead of standing through the wettest hurling match in history. I am sure it has earned that distinction.

With a river of rain running down the back of my neck and my hat in ruins about my face, and a stream of water rushing up my sleeves, and a perfect Niagara descending into my shoes, I just hated every moment of it....

I was ploughing about in the mud and puddles for quite a long time before I got hoisted on some steps behind the sideline. From my perch I looked down on a great sloping, solid wall of humanity which encircled the entire field. Upon this scene a heavy grey sky, so low that it seemed to rest on the red roof of the Hogan Stand, sent down a myriad spears of silver water in a steady downpour. Spears! They were swords — and as surely as swords they cut through the garments of the crowds until you could see that their very underwear was sticking to their skin.

To a man and a woman who were so thrilled with the game that for all they cared it might have been the finest day of the year. Yet there were times when the players were at the opposite goal that one could hardly see them through the rain.

The players were a magnificent looking set of men, all of them powerfully built. They kept their feet on the slippery ground like skaters on a rink. There were very few tosses, and it was as fine and clean and equally matched game as anyone could wish to see.

When it proved so thrilling a contest in the pouring rain, what would not it have been on a fine day?

Towards the end of the game yesterday, when one side or another scored a goal, strong, silent businessmen, serious farmers, decorous professional men would jump out of their seats onto the grass and catch each other round the waist and dance round, or jump a foot in the air, wildly waving umbrellas or flags, or spring up and down a number of times, the while yelling so madly and so hoarsely that eventually their voices would crack demoniacally on a too-high note.

It was astounding to see fathers of families, and even grandfathers, behaving like this, then quickly returning to their seats when they realised that they were missing the game.

Women get just as excited about it; but they are far quieter in their demonstrations and more frightened of appearing foolish.

Every now and again the heavy downpour would develop into a storm of rain that rattled down on us with the noise of pebbles and in drops the size of pebbles. The onslaughts of water came quite frequently.

One reason why men enjoy a hurling match so much is, I think, that it gives them such a glorious opportunity of offering advice.

I first spied 'Kilkenny' in the crowd moving along below the steps on which I was standing, and I was overcome with pity for him. He had neither raincoat nor hat and his thin Summer suit was so soaked that you would think he had just been dragged from a river. He wore a white handkerchief knotted over his head, his face was ashy and he was visibly shaking with cold.

I lost sight of him in the crowd, and the next time I saw him he was standing on the step beside me, a rivulet of water pouring down his nose. But now his shivers were gone and he was yelling like one demented. When he had given a series of jumps over a Kilkenny goal and finished with a prolonged blood-curling roar that seemed to come out of the back of his head, I looked apprehensively at the New Zealander below me, and fervently hoped that he didn't think it was some sort of native dance — such as a Maori war dance.

'Go on, Kilkenny, hook him in the neck', he yelled. 'Good man, Larkin, ye beauty! That's the stuff to give them, Kilkenny, you're all over them. Go on, Lahy (Leahy), show them how to hurl. Dumn good puck! That's the stuff to give them, son. Come on, Kilkenny, walk over them'.

This last injunction ended in a yell that ought to have split his head, but it didn't. Then he wilted a bit. The time was growing short and anything might happen. Kilkenny scored a point.

'Points is no good', he exclaimed despondently.

There was a Kilkenny supporter on the other side of him. This one wore his cap from back to front and was not nearly so vocal.

Still minutes to go, and if the game could stop then all would be well for Kilkenny. 'Bet my boots it's full time', said the white handkerchief not too hopefully.

'Ach', exclaimed the man with the cap, vocal at last, 'it's the longest half hour in Ireland'.

But it came to an end, and it was worth waiting for, I decided after all.

They are two great teams and they played yesterday to the rhythm of a great slogan. It was printed at the foot of the programme in Gaelic:

'Purity of our hearts,
Strength of our Limbs,
Deeds to match our words'

'Glaine ár gcroí 'gus neart ár ngéag,
Is beart de réir ar mbriathar'

Osborn Ó h-Aimhirgin.
From the poem 'Trí Tréithe Na Féinne'

The 1911 title opened the door to three in a row for Kilkenny — the only time these great artists of the game achieved such an honour. When it was completed, in 1913, there ended a most glorious era in Kilkenny hurling.

Pierce Grace was part of those three hurling triumphs. Earlier, in 1906 and 1907, he had played for Dublin when they won All-Ireland football titles, and was the first man to win more than one All-Ireland medal in both hurling and football. He was followed by Frank Burke, a native of Kildare who, unlike Pierce, won his medals with the same county (his adopted Dublin) — hurling: 1917 and 1920; football: 1921, 1922 and 1923.

To date no other player has had such a level of success. Neither has there been a walk-over final.

THE RARE FOUR-IN-A-ROW ALL-IRELAND ACHIEVEMENTS

In the history of the Gaelic Athletic Association, the tremendous achievement of four-in-a-row All-Ireland senior titles has occurred on only four occasions.

The men of Wexford were the first to achieve the honour. Their footballers won the title every year from 1915 to 1918 inclusive, thus setting a standard that would be hard to follow and exceedingly difficult to surpass.

Kerry footballers reached that standard in the years 1929 to 1932, and from 1941 to 1944 the magic four was achieved by the Cork hurlers.

It would be thirty-four years before another band of men would emerge to write their county into the record books. This time it was Kerry footballers again. In 1981, almost half a century after their forefathers, they won their fourth All-Ireland senior title in a row.

One for Wexford. One for Cork. Two for Kerry. It is interesting to look at each of these achievements in greater detail.

Wexford, 1915–1918

Wexford's march to fame began with Leinster title victories over Louth in 1913 and 1914. The Wexfordmen fell to Kerry in the 1913 All-Ireland final by 5 points, but the following year they drew on the first day. The 15,000 spectators were treated to a thrilling and exciting game on a pitch made heavy by the torrential rain of the previous day. Harry Boland was in charge of the whistle, and the Wexford display was marked by speed, strength and combination. They were a point ahead with a minute to go when Dick Fitzgerald was fouled at the 21-yards line. Silence gripped the crowd as he approached the greasy ball — and made no mistake with the equaliser. According to the journalist 'Carbery', 'It was Greek meeting Greek in that last quarter-hour through the gathering dusk'. Four weeks later, on 29 November, Wexford lost the replay by three points, but great days lay ahead.

For the next four years Wexford were the finest football combination in the land. They were captained by the New Ross stalwart athlete, Seán O'Kennedy, in the successive victories of 1915, 1916 and 1917. O'Kennedy was the only man with such a senior record. A dual player of rare ability, he played for Leinster in the Railway Shield in hurling and football, and was fullback on the 1910 All-Ireland winning Wexford senior hurling team. Alas, major surgery deprived him of leading his native Wexford to a fourth All-Ireland football title in 1918. Jim Byrne of Wexford took over the mantle of captain.

Nine players had the honour of participating in all four All-Ireland winning teams: Jim Byrne, Gus O'Kennedy, Martin Howlett, Rich Reynolds, Aidan Doyle, Tom Doyle (Tearin' Tom), Tom Murphy, Tom McGrath and Paddy Mackey.

Like Seán O'Kennedy, Paddy Mackey also distinguished himself as a dual performer. Born in The Rower, Co. Kilkenny — just a few miles outside New Ross — he became eligible for Wexford by residing in New Ross. Between his four-in-a-row football titles, and his All-Ireland hurling medal of 1910, he won a total of five All-Ireland senior medals.

Surprisingly, although Wexford's first game in defence of their Leinster title in 1915 was against Kilkenny, it was played in Waterford. Victory over Offaly in the next round set the scene for a Leinster final meeting with Dublin. It went to a replay on Sunday, 10 October, before Wexford won by 3:5 to 1:3. The referee was Pat Dunphy of Laois. Both games attracted a combined attendance of almost 25,000 supporters, and gate receipts of £575 created a record at the time.

Cavan fell at the semi-final, so for the third year in a row it was Wexford v Kerry in the football final — and the question on all footballing lips was whether Wexford could, at the third attempt, defeat mighty Kerry led by Dick Fitzgerald.

When Pat Dunphy of Laois blew the final whistle on 7 November, the answer to that question was known. And the answer was yes. The score read Wexford 2:4; Kerry 2:1 — a famous victory. Both teams served up a powerful display of excellent, robust football in a great final that generated immense excitement and enthusiasm in the 30,000 spectators who had paid a total of £1,044 at the gate. Ideal weather conditions, a good sod and a fine sporting spirit added greatly to the occasion. Wexford led at the interval by 1:2 to a goal. Their goal had come at a crucial stage, just before half time, following a swift passing movement between Gus O'Kennedy, Rich Reynolds and Aidan Doyle. But the goal that won the match came about ten minutes from the end when — to the consternation of the Kerrymen — Wexford defender Jim Byrne sent a thirty-yards free all the way to the Kerry net, just under the crossbar.

Every Wexfordman was a hero. Kerry — perceived in many quarters to be invincible — had had their colours lowered.

Wexford were now experienced and seasoned performers. Victory gave them an added confidence and they faced the 1916 campaign as favourites. Then two things happened that further enhanced their All-Ireland prospects. First, Dublin failed to field a team to fulfil their first-round engagement with Wexford at Wexford Park. This was followed by the sensational news that Kerry had withdrawn from the championship, following a dispute with the Central Council over the question of expenses. So, before a ball was kicked, the two teams that held the greatest threat for Wexford were gone.

Wexford reached the All-Ireland final with victories over Meath, Kildare and Monaghan. The last of these games created a bit of GAA history. Monaghan were an emerging power in Ulster and had surprised many with their 3:1 to 0:2 win over Cavan. When Wexford agreed to travel to Carrickmacross for the game, it was the first time an All-Ireland semi-final was played in Ulster. Wexford's sporting gesture was deeply appreciated and they received a tremendous reception from the Northern followers.

A shock result seemed a distinct possibility for the crowd of 5,000 at half-time when the score read Wexford 0:5; Monaghan 1:1. But it wasn't to be. Monaghan didn't score in the second half and Wexford finished the hour 0:9 to 1:1.

The All-Ireland final against Mayo took place on 17 December — the closest to Christmas Day ever played. The attendance of fewer than 3,000 was one of the smallest ever. Wexford won by 3:4 to 1:2, but were not flattered by the margin of victory as it didn't reflect their superiority. That made it two in a row — their third title in all, having defeated Cork in 1893. Over a four-year period they had demonstrated that they were the most consistent team in Ireland — they were now the team everyone wanted to beat. It was with that reputation that Wexford faced 1917.

Victories over Wicklow and Westmeath took Wexford to a Leinster final meeting with old rivals, Dublin. The match was played before a crowd of 7,000 people, and R. Rogers of Louth was in charge of the whistle. With three minutes remaining, the score read Dublin 1:1; Wexford 0:3. It looked as if Wexford were about to make an exit from the championship — the end of an era? But another piece of Wexford football magic involving ace-freetaker Jim Byrne and inspirational captain Seán O'Kennedy saw Aidan Doyle finish the ball to the Dublin net. It was a close call, but champions survive close calls. Wexford were Leinster champions for the fifth year in a row. With Kerry again refusing to compete in 1917, Wexford were now firm favourites to take the title for the third year in succession.

They confirmed that rating with a resounding 6:6 to 1:3 victory over Ulster champions, Monaghan, who returned the compliment of the previous year by travelling to Wexford Park for the game. A crowd of 7,000 left the grounds convinced they had seen the 1917 champions in action. And they were right.

In the final, Wexford met Clare, who reached the decider with wins over Waterford — 2:6 to 0:3, Tipperary — 5 points to 4, Cork — 5:4 to 0:1, and Galway — 2:1 to 0:4. The match took place at Croke Park on 9 December. It was a tough physical game but Wexford held a tight grip on proceedings and emerged as champions for the third year in a row on the score 0:9 to 0:5. A well-known name in the Clare line-out was Tull Considine who subsequently excelled as a hurler.

Wexford had now equalled Dublin's previously unbeaten three-in-a-row record. Dublin had had three-in-a row wins in the years 1897 to 1899 and again from 1906 to 1908.

Wexford had a chance to set a new record in 1918. This was a difficult year in Ireland. The political situation led to the British military authorities banning all Gaelic games except under permit — a move that was strenuously resisted. In defiance of the order, the GAA nominated Sunday, 4 August, as Gaelic Sunday and arranged for almost 1,000 games to be played throughout the country. There was little police interference.

Following an act passed in the British House of Commons, the question of conscription reared its head in Ireland. It met with fierce opposition from laity and clergy, and further fuelled political unrest.

The general unease and disquiet in the country were augmented by the flu epidemic which took a heavy toll and cost many lives. Yet, despite all, Wexford reached both senior finals. Their hurlers lost heavily to a brilliant Limerick team in a final played at Croke Park on 26 January 1919, with 10,000 supporters in attendance.

However, the Wexford footballers made history. In Leinster they defeated Kilkenny 2:6 to 0:1, Carlow, and Louth 2:5 to 1:4 to take their sixth in a row provincial title.

Their opponents in the All-Ireland final were a highly fancied Tipperary team. They came with good credentials, having had victories over Cork — 1:3 to 0:3, Waterford — 4:4 to nil, Kerry — 1:1 to 0:1, and, somewhat luckily, Mayo — 2:2 to 1:4.

The final, which took place at Croke Park on 16 February 1919 before a crowd of 10,000 supporters, was one of the best finals for some years. Close throughout, it was played at a fast pace and there was some really good football. The closeness of the scoring made the game a cliff-hanger. At half time, it was anybody's game, with Wexford holding a slender 1-point lead — 3 points to 2. It was level pegging with ten minutes to go but shortly before the end Wexford produced the winning point. Although it was a low-scoring game — 5 points to 4 — the result spelt glory and renown for the model county. However, it was to be the end of the road for them in the field of All-Ireland senior football success.

Wexford's fifth All-Ireland football title was their fourth in a row. It was also the first-ever four in a row — a benchmark. A standard had been set, which would be hard to follow — even more difficult to surpass.

WEXFORD		1915 VKERRY	1916 VMAYO	1917 VCLARE	1918 VTIPPERARY
Sean Kennedy	1	✓ c	✓ c	✓ c	—
Gus Kennedy	2	✓	✓	✓	✓
Paddy Mackey	3	✓	✓	✓	✓
Tom Murphy	4	✓	✓	✓	✓
Frank Furlong	5	✓	✓	✓	—
Tom Wall	6	✓	✓	—	—
Fr E. Wheeler	7	✓ alias Jas Furlong	✓	✓ alias J. Quinn	—
Tom Mernagh	8	✓	✓	✓	—
Tom Doyle	9	✓	✓	✓	✓
Ed Black	10	✓	—	—	—
Aidan Doyle	11	✓	✓	✓	✓
Jim Byrne	12	✓	✓	✓	✓ c
Martin Howlett	13	✓	✓	✓	✓
Rich Reynolds	14	✓	✓	✓	✓
Tom McGrath	15	✓	✓	✓	✓
Jack Crowley	16	—	✓	✓	✓
W. Hodgins	17	—	—	✓	✓
Nick Stuart	18	—	—	—	✓
John Doran	19	—	—	—	✓
Toddy Pierse	20	—	—	—	✓
Jim Redmond	21	—	—	—	✓

Nine played in all four finals
c — captain

	v	v	v	v
	Kilkenny 0.9: 0.4	Dublin w/o	Wicklow 6.4: 0.2	Kilkenny 2.6: 0.1
	Offaly 1.7: 0.2	Meath 6.5: 1.2	W'meath 1.7: 0.1	Carlow
	Dublin 2.2: 2.2	Kildare 1.7:1.0	Dublin 1.3: 1.1	Louth 2.5: 1.4
	Dublin 3.5: 1.3	Mon.* 0.9: 1.1	Mon. 6.6: 1.3	Tipperary 0.5: 0.4
	Cavan 3.7: 2.2	Mayo 3.4: 1.2	Clare 0.9: 0.5	
	Kerry 2.4: 2.1			
	* Mon. = Monaghan			

Kerry, 1929–1932

The 1923 final, played on 28 September 1924, saw Kerry appear in their first All-Ireland final since 1915. They met Dublin, the football kingpins of that era, and lost by 1:5 to 1:3. Dublin — playing in their fourth-in-a-row final — made it a third win in a row. They were backboned by Frank Burke, the McDonalds — Paddy and Johnny — and the Synnotts — John and Josie.

It was one of the great football finals. Croke Park was packed to capacity long before the throw-in. Twenty-nine special trains brought football fans to the capital. Kerrymen — ranged on opposite sides in the tragic Civil War — fought for a common cause in the green and gold jersey. A healing process was in progress.

Among the great Kerry names that would live in the annals of the football immortals were Con Brosnan, Paul Russell, Joe Barrett and John Joe Sheehy — a footballing colossus of speed, strength and leadership qualities, who was honoured in the Hall of Fame by Texaco in 1963.

Con Brosnan's first-half goal in 1923 gave Kerry hope but it wasn't enough. Nonetheless, they were on the march and were to become the team of the decade — though closely followed by Kildare.

The 1924 final was played on 26 April 1925 as the GAA tried to bring all championships up to date. Kerry and Dublin were again the contestants. Thirty special trains ferried supporters to the capital. A crowd of 28,000 people were treated to what Sliabh Ruadh described as 'a hard, vigorous contest' in one of the lowest-scoring finals on record — Kerry 0:4; Dublin 0:3.

(The strange events of 1925 are dealt with in the chapter entitled 'The Football Final Fiasco 1925' — pp 47–9.)

The finals of 1926 and 1927 between Kerry and Kildare evoked memories of the classic games between the same counties when they had clashed in 1903 and 1905. Crowds of up to 40,000 flocked to see the cream of Ireland's footballers in action. Gate receipts touched the £3,400 mark for each game. The football was superb. The pace was terrific. Kerry won in 1926 on 17 October — 1:4 to 0:4 — following a 1:3 to 0:6 draw on the first Sunday in September. Kildare avenged their defeat in 1927, winning by 5 points to 3 points.

Joe Barrett   *John Joe Sheehy*

Kerry's football ambitions suffered a surprise, but temporary, set-back in the Munster semi-final of 1928, when they went under to Tipperary at Tipperary Town on the score 2:1 to 2 goals.

Kerry had moulded a superb combination. They were fit, experienced, well practised. They had speed and durability. It's not surprising that they won four National League titles in a row — 1927/28, 1928/29, 1930/31 and 1931/32.

All of the foregoing set the scene for the events of 1929 to 1932.

Many of the men on the Kerry team had already played in four All-Ireland finals — losing in 1923 and 1927, winning in 1924 and 1926. The big time did not faze them — in fact, they revelled in it.

They met their famed rivals, Kildare, in the final of 1929. Again they drew the crowds, with 43,000 fans in attendance, and record gate receipts of £4,010. It was a great game, the final score of which was Kerry 1:8; Kildare 1:5.

'Sliabh Ruadh' reported as follows: 'The vigour and determination of the Munster men proved too much for the less forceful if more polished game of Kildare'.

In 1930 Monaghan emerged from Ulster, having defeated a fancied Cavan fifteen. They then accounted for Kildare in the All-Ireland semi-final with a good two-point win. However, they were completely overawed by the experience of final-day, and a rampant Kerry had the easiest of wins — 3:11 to 0:2.

Sadly, celebrations were muted as a great Kerry Gael had passed away on 26 September — the Friday before the final. He was Dick Fitzgerald of Killarney, a footballing legend who had captained Kerry to All-Ireland victories in 1913 and 1914.

'Sliabh Ruadh' mourned his passing and wrote a lament which includes the following lines:

> *Over Loch Lein, where the sad moon pales,*
> *Rises a caoine for a chief of the Gaels,*
> *A Leader gone from the fighting line —*
> *A scion true of the Geraldine!*
> *Through the mist of years his name will gleam,*
> *When he blazed the trail with his Kerry team,*
> *And brought to the 'Kingdom' name and fame*
> *In the greatest tests of the Gaelic game;*
> *Kildare and Wexford and Louth can tell*
> *Of his deeds, and now his requiem swell,*
> *And tribute pay to a gallant foe,*
> *Who played the game as we Gaels know.*
> *And now he's gone from the field of fame,*
> *But thousands still shall speak his name,*
> *And tell of his deed on the Gaelic field*
> *For the Irish crown and the Railway Shield.*

The 1930 Kerry team made history on St Patrick's Day 1931. With one change from the All-Ireland winning team — Tim Landers for Jas Baily — they represented Munster in the Railway Cup final and defeated Leinster by 2:2 to 6 points, thus renewing rivalries with seven Kildare men, in 'one of the finest displays of the native code ever witnessed at headquarters'.

In May, this great band of footballers set off on a successful American tour, the highlight of which was the victory over New York at Yankee Stadium before an attendance of 50,000 supporters.

The year 1931 saw the fourth meeting (since 1926) of Kerry and Kildare in the football finals. Sadly, it was the last time these counties were to contest the final in the twentieth century. Each time they met, they produced a thrilling spectacle of Gaelic football. They had peerless names in their ranks and, with grand hands and great footwork, they were masters of the art of catch and kick. In what proved to be another memorable encounter for an attendance of almost 43,000 spectators, Kerry won by

1:11 to 0:8, making four wins for Kerry, two for Kildare, in their six meetings.

Dan O'Keeffe made his début in goal for Kerry in 1931. He was to play in ten All-Ireland finals and win seven medals. He was one of football's greatest goalkeepers.

Much of note occurred in the Ireland of 1932. On the political front, Fianna Fáil came to power, following a General Election in February. The Eucharistic Congress was held in Ireland in June and it is estimated that about a million people attended the concluding Mass in the Phoenix Park, one of the outstanding features of which was the great John McCormack's rendition of 'Panis Angelicus'. The fifteenth centenary of the coming of St Patrick was also celebrated in that year.

On the sporting front, the last of the Tailteann games were held by the GAA — the third of a four-year series that were revived in 1924. Meanwhile, on an international level, Ireland won fame and honour at the Olympic games in Los Angeles with Dr Pat O'Callaghan and Bob Tisdall winning gold medals for hammer throwing and 440-yard hurdles respectively.

In spite of these causes for celebration, all was not well in the economic field. The shock waves of the world depression were being felt, and many factories closed. Unemployment rose sharply and the prices of both livestock and dairy produce slumped.

Gaelic games provided a diversion. The football public's speculation as to whether Kerry could emulate the men of Wexford and make it a historic four in a row was rewarded with a final victory over Mayo. Despite being in arrears at half time, Kerry won by 2:7 to 2:4.

For the Landers family it was an occasion for extra special celebration. Tim and John Joe lined out for the throw-in, and Bill, who had won a medal in 1924, came on as a substitute. In 1937 John Joe added a fifth medal to his four in a row, while Tim, who was on the winning teams of 1931 and 1932, added three more medals in 1937, 1939 and 1941 when he came on to play as a sub.

The four-in-a-row was a wonderful achievement. Ten players were architects of all four successes — Joe Barrett, Jack Walsh, Paul Russell, Con Brosnan, Bob Stack, Jackie Ryan, 'Dee'

O'Connor, Joe O'Sullivan, Miko Doyle and John Joe Landers. And for the first six of these it was a sixth All-Ireland medal.

KERRY		1929 v KILDARE	1930 v MONAGHAN	1931 v KILDARE	1932 v MAYO
Johnny Riordan	1	✓	✓	—	—
'Dee' O'Connor	2	✓	✓	✓	✓
Joe Barrett	3	✓ c	✓	✓	✓ c
Jack Walsh	4	✓	✓	✓	✓
Paul Russell	5	✓	✓	✓	✓
Joe O'Sullivan	6	✓	✓	✓	✓
Tim O'Donnell	7	✓	✓	—	—
Con Brosnan	8	✓	✓	✓ c	✓
Bob Stack	9	✓	✓	✓	✓
Jackie Ryan	10	✓	✓	✓	✓
Miko Doyle	11	✓	✓	✓	✓
John Joe Landers	12	✓	✓	✓	✓
Ned Sweeney	13	✓	✓	—	—
Jas Baily	14	✓	—	—	—
John Joe Sheehy	15	✓	✓ c	—	—
Eamon Fitzgerald	16	—	✓	✓	—
Dan O'Keeffe	17	—	—	✓	✓
Tim Landers	18	—	—	✓	✓
Paddy Whitty	19	—	—	✓	✓
M. Regan	20	—	—	✓	—
Johnny Walsh	21	—	—	—	✓
C. Geaney	22	—	—	—	✓
Bill Landers	23	—	—	—	sub
Ten played in all four finals					
c — captain					
sub — came on as a substitute during the match					

Joe Barrett was captain in 1929 and 1932. John Joe Sheehy had the honour in 1930, having also led Kerry to success in 1926. The leader in 1931 was Con Brosnan.

Kerrymen Dick Fitzgerald (left) and Dan O'Keeffe (right)

In all, twenty-three players participated in the four finals as the table on p. 124 shows.

Most of the men of that era were 'Hall of Fame' material. They played direct football — no frills, no fancy stuff. They were masterly in the art of high fielding, followed by long accurate kicking. The team was a football machine. The year 1932 was the end of an era, but by no means the last great era in Kerry football.

Cork, 1941–1944

When the final whistle sounded on 1 November 1931, after the second replay against Kilkenny, a victorious Cork team brought to an end a great Cork hurling era. It took seven games to clinch the title — first Clare, then Tipperary, a draw and replay against Waterford in the Munster final, and a piece of hurling history with three games against Kilkenny in the All-Ireland final.

In 1926, 1928 and 1929 Cork powered their way to All-Ireland success. Their semi-final win of 5:3 to 0:2 over Dublin in 1928 suggests that they may have been 'caught' in the 1927 final by what admittedly was a great Dublin team — backboned by the famous Garda team and tremendously fit. Jim Regan, the great Cork centre half-back of those days, was contemplating a £10 bet on Cork against Dublin, in 1928, when a Dublin mentor told him that Dublin were better than they had been the previous year. Jim changed his mind but regretted it when the final whistle blew.

In 1930, Cork lost to Clare by one goal in the Munster semi-final. In the six years from 1926 to 1931 inclusive, Cork won four All-Ireland titles. They might have made it four in a row in any of those six years. However, that glory had to wait for another day and for other men.

After 1931, there followed a lengthy barren patch for Cork. In 1939 they surfaced again and had the better of it in a hectic and superb Munster final against Limerick, with just two points between them after sixty minutes of breathtaking hurling. But their hour had not yet come and, in what was to become known as 'the thunder and lightning All-Ireland final', Kilkenny shaded it by just one point. When Limerick avenged the 1939 defeat the following year, in a Munster final that left spectators gasping and scribes groping for descriptive superlatives, Cork were left wondering about the future. But the two years had shown that the raw material was very good, though nobody could have envisaged what lay ahead.

In the years 1941–1944, as Europe was torn asunder in a savage World War, Cork proved themselves to be the finest hurling team in the land. They won four All-Ireland hurling titles in a row. No hurling team had previously done it. By the turn of the century, none had matched it.

The chart shows that Cork used 28 players between all four finals. Nine had the distinction of playing in all four: Willie Murphy, Batt Thornhill, Alan Lotty, Din Joe Buckley, Jim Young, Johnny Quirke, Jack Lynch, Christy Ring and Paddy O'Donovan who came on as a substitute in 1941 and 1943.

The finals themselves were easily won as the scores indicate:

1941 v Dublin — 5:11 to 0:6
1942 v Dublin — 2:14 to 3:4
1943 v Antrim — 5:16 to 0:4
1944 v Dublin — 2:13 to 1:2

The thrills and spills and narrow escapes took place in the early rounds.

For example, in 1941 there was an outbreak of foot-and-mouth disease, which threw the championships into disarray. Limerick accounted for Clare in the first round — a semi-final — and qualified for the Munster final. Tipperary defeated Waterford in Thurles in a game that was originally fixed for 1 June but was postponed until 27 July. The date for the semi-final meeting of Tipperary and Cork was set as 17 August, at Limerick. But six days before, following a directive from the Department of Agriculture, the game was called off. A decision was then taken by the Munster Council that Cork and Limerick should meet to decide who would represent Munster in the All-Ireland final. The game, which took place at Cork on 14 September, was never likely to match the memorable Munster final meeting of 1939 and the epic draw and replay in the Munster final of 1940 between these two great rivals. Missing from the Limerick line-out were the Mackey brothers, Mick and John — following a family bereavement — and Paddy Clohessy, outstanding centre half-back of the time, who, at 31, had retired prematurely. It was one-way traffic. Cork won 8:10 to 3:2 and progressed to the All-Ireland final, having played just one game.

In Leinster, as Tom Ryall records in his book *Kilkenny the GAA Story 1884–1984*:

> Kilkenny were drawn against Laois in the first round, but because of the foot-and-mouth outbreak, they could not play and were given a bye into the Leinster final. The Department of Agriculture brought out an order that Kilkenny could not play in the Leinster final, until the county was three weeks clear of foot-and-mouth. The result was that Dublin were nominated to represent Leinster in the All-Ireland semi-final.

Dublin eliminated Galway at Roscrea on the second Sunday in September but proved no match for Cork in the final on 28 September. The final score read Cork 5:11; Dublin 0:6

The delayed Leinster final was played in November at Croke Park where Dublin defeated Kilkenny 2:8 to 1:8. The delayed Munster final was played at Limerick on 26 October, and brought a shock result — Tipperary 5:4; Cork 2:5.

A unique situation was thus created, with Tipperary the Munster champions of 1941, but Cork the All-Ireland champions. And it took only two games. The 1941 hurling title must surely rank as the easiest All-Ireland senior crown ever won.

The best game of the 1942 hurling championship was at Limerick Gaelic grounds, where the Munster semi-final between Cork and Limerick was played. It proved to be Cork's greatest test of the season. In a game of hectic and scintillating hurling, with thrills heaped on thrills, Cork got their two winning points in extra time. The late Jim Young, playing at wing-back that day for Cork, remembered it as the greatest game of hurling he ever played in during his long career — and he played in many great ones.

Waterford presented the greatest obstacle in 1943. They had some grand hurlers: Jim Ware, John Keane, Christy Moylan, Andy Fleming, Mick Hayes and Mick Hickey. Cork were glad to hear the final whistle on that August Sunday when they survived by just two points, 2:13 to 3:8. They had retained their Munster crown.

In 1944, Cork were made earn their All-Ireland title. It was by far their toughest campaign in their search for four in a row. They weren't unduly extended in their 1:9 to 1:3 win over Tipperary — a win that gave them a place in the Munster final against Limerick.

Patrons expected a thriller from the Cork v Limerick match. And they got it. In fact, they got a double helping because there was a draw and a replay.

In Europe, war still raged but the tide of battle was favouring the Allies. In Ireland, Emergency conditions had put private cars off the road, and to use any petrol-driven vehicle for transport to matches was strictly forbidden. Accordingly, every other mode of transport was used — pony and trap, sidecars, common cars, but most of all, the bicycle. They converged on Thurles from all angles — and from as far away as Antrim — some perspiring as weary legs felt the pressure. And the procession stretched for miles and miles as they pedalled their way into Thurles like ants on the move. Many set forth on Saturday, among them big Jim Hurley of Cork, star performer of the 1920s and 1930s. And there were those with no form of transport who walked from as far away as forty miles. In the Mick Mackey story, it is recorded

Jack Lynch with Micka Brennan and Johnny Quirke

that 'sixty-five-years-old Peter Ryan set off from Lisnagry, walking 35 miles to see the game'. He, like the others, had come to watch the cream of Ireland's hurling men in action. And Thurles pitch on those two July Sundays abounded with great names — immortal hurling sons, such as Christy Ring and Mick Mackey, Timmy Ryan and Jack Lynch, Johnny Quirke and John Mackey, Jim Young and Dick Stokes, Jackie Power and Willie Murphy, Peter Cregan and Din Joe Buckley, Seán Herbert and Willie Campbell, Con Murphy, Alan Lotty, Seán Condon and Batt Thornhill.

It was very, very close for Cork, but surviving is the stuff of champions. In the drawn game, with extra time being played, the scoreboard read Limerick 4:12; Cork 5:7 — Cork were two points down. Then veteran Johnny Quirke engineered the greatest goal of his long career for Cork. Now 4:12 to 6:7 for Cork. A point to the good. On the call of time, Dick Stokes got the equaliser for Limerick. 'Carbery' described it as 'a final that had a heart-throbbing pulsating finish that took people's breath away ... carrying all the fire and brilliancy of the great Munster hurling finals of the past'.

The replay two weeks later, on 30 July, was even more epic and dramatic. Extra time is being played. The score reads

Limerick 3:6; Cork 3:5. The crowd are in a frenzy. Again to the rescue comes the stout-hearted Johnny Quirke with a lovely swing and a beautiful point. A draw it seems, and extra time as the referee looks at his watch. But Ring is away at speed on a solo run and his shot deceives backs and forwards as it finishes in the Limerick net. The drama continues as Mackey at the other end, in search of an equaliser, knocks the lime off the upright on the wrong side. Full time. Cork march on.

'Carbery' summed it up well: 'it will rank with the classic Munster finals of the past — in its stern naked grandeur, in its hearty manly spirit where rival surging bloods swing ash with freedom and abandon'.

The semi-final against Galway at Ennis was a tough, gruelling affair. Without the services, through injury, of Jack Lynch and Johnny Quirke, it was Cork's experience and cohesion that brought them through against a hard-hitting and talented Galway outfit. It couldn't have been closer — Cork 1:10; Galway 3:3.

The final against Dublin turned out to be a formality. Cork were All-Ireland champions. They made hurling history — four in a row. Great men all.

Cork Team
Back Row: *(left to right) J. Barry (trainer), C. Buckley, M. Brennan, A. Lotty, J. Lynch, B. Thornhill, J. Barrett, T. O'Sullivan, 'Bowler' Walsh (Cork County Board).* **Middle Row:** *(left to right) W. Campbell, D.J. Buckley, J. Buttimer, J. Quirke, W. Murphy, J. Young.* **Seated:** *C. Ring, C. Cottrell.*

CORK		1941 v DUBLIN	1942 v DUBLIN	1943 v ANTRIM	1944 v DUBLIN
Jim Buttimer	1	✓	✓ sub	—	—
Willie Murphy	2	✓ ●	✓ ●	✓ ●	✓ ●
Batt Thornhill	3	✓	✓ ●	✓	✓
Alan Lotty	4	✓ ●	✓	✓	✓
Willie Campbell	5	✓ ●	—	—	—
Con Cottrell	6	✓	—	✓	✓ ●
Din Joe Buckley	7	✓	✓	✓	✓
Jim Young	8	✓	✓	✓ ●	✓ ●
Johnny Quirke	9	✓ ●	✓ ●	✓ ●	✓ ●
Ted O'Sullivan	10	✓	—	✓	—
Micka Brennan	11	✓	—	✓	—
J. Ryng	12	✓ sub	—	—	—
Paddy O'Donovan	13	✓ sub	✓	✓ sub	✓
Ned Porter	14	—	✓	—	—
Con Murphy	15	—	✓	✓	✓
Sean Barrett	16	✓	—	—	—
Jack Lynch	17	✓ ●	✓ c ●	✓ ●	✓ ●
Christy Ring	18	✓	✓ ●	✓ ●	✓ ●
Sean Condon	19	—	✓	✓	✓ c ●
Mick Kennifick	20	—	✓	✓ c	—
Charlie Tobin	21	—	✓	—	—
Derry Beckett	22	—	✓	—	—
Connie Buckley	23	✓ c ●	—	—	—
Tom Mulcahy	24	—	—	✓	✓
Bernie Murphy	25	—	—	✓ sub	—
Jim Morrison	26	—	—	—	✓
Joe Kelly	27	—	—	—	✓
Paddy Healy	28	—	—	—	✓ sub

Nine played in all four finals

● — *Selected for Munster in Railway Cup*

c — *captain*

sub — *came on as a substitute during the match*

Kerry, 1978–1981

Kerry's second four-in-a-row achievement, from 1978 to 1981 inclusive, fits neatly into the centre of a wonderful twelve-year spell in Kerry football history. It had a strong Limerick connection in the persons of Ger Power, Eoin Liston and Denis 'Ogie' Moran. Remarkably, during that long spell, Kerry's footballing giants never lost their zestful appetite for the game, and there were many highlights in those dozen years from 1975 to 1986.

In 1975 a very young and unsung Kerry team arrived on the scene. They took the Gaelic football world by storm. Trained to the ounce, under coach Mick O'Dwyer, they played at high speed. It was precision football, involving sweeping movements out of defence and delightful forward play of well-nigh faultless combination, which baffled and mesmerised many an opposing back line.

Victories over Tipperary, Cork, Sligo and Dublin saw them crowned All-Ireland champions. Their captain, Micky O'Sullivan, following a very dangerous double-tackle midway through the first half, was concussed and removed to hospital where he was detained overnight. In his absence, Pat Spillane collected the Sam Maguire Cup. It was the first time in the history of the game that the winning captain was unable to accept Sam.

The 1975 victory was a prelude to great days. In 1976 and 1977, Kerry would undergo a maturing process — losing to Dublin by seven points in the 1976 final, and by five points in the All-Ireland semi-final of 1977. The latter was a game that ranks among the greatest of all time — one of the classics.

In the twelve-year period in question, Kerry won every Munster title except that of 1983. That year, they were ahead by two points as players and spectators awaited the final whistle. A far-out harmless-looking free to Cork was quickly taken and, in a twinkling, Tadhg Murphy had the ball in the net. At full time, Kerry had missed a record-breaking nine in a row in Munster.

Kerry won the National League titles of 1977, 1982 and 1984. Munster contested nine Railway Cup finals between the years 1975 and 1986, and won six. In 1981, there were thirteen Kerrymen on the Munster team. All-Star awards accumulated by

Kerry players during the same period reached the remarkable figure of sixty-five.

During those twelve years, Kerry contested ten All-Ireland finals — missing out only in 1977, when they lost the semi-final to Dublin, and 1983 when Cork beat them in the Munster final.

Of the ten finals contested, Kerry won eight. They lost to Dublin in 1976 and Offaly in 1982. That year it seemed as if they had a record-breaking five in a row all sown up despite having a penalty saved by the great Martin Furling in the Offaly goal. In the dying moments, a free to Offaly from around midfield did not suggest that the Kerry citadel was under threat, but the movement from it saw Seamus Darby, who had come in as a substitute, score a super goal. It came at a crucial moment, and 'twas worth a King's ransom. It rocked the mighty kingdom. Offaly collected a third title. A Kerry dream evaporated.

It is sometimes forgotten that Kerry had also come very close to a five-in-a-row All-Ireland success in the period from 1937 to 1941. The Munster finals presented no great difficulty as the following scorelines indicate:

1937 v Clare — 4:9 to 1:1

1938 v Cork — 4:14 to 0:6

1939 v Tipperary — 2:11 to 0:4

1940 v Waterford — 1:10 to 0:6

1941 v Clare — 2:9 to 0:6

E. Walsh

Their only All-Ireland loss was in 1938 to Galway — in a final that went to a replay. The 1937 and 1938 campaigns are dealt with in the chapter entitled 'The All-Ireland Football Final Draws' — pp 139–55.

The closing stages of the three subsequent campaigns were close, tough and demanding. It took two semi-final games in 1939 to dispose of Mayo. The final against Meath was a very close affair. Meath, appearing in their second All-Ireland final — their first since 1895 — and backboned by the Donnellys, Matt O'Toole and 'Boiler' McGuinness, gave a wonderful account of themselves. They matched the vaunted Kerrymen in all facets of the game but had to give way in the end on the score 2:5 to 2:3. Kerry captain, Tom O'Connor, took Sam to the kingdom once more.

Time was ticking away in the All-Ireland final of 1940 against Galway. Scores were level at 6 points to 1:3. The Kerry captain, Dan Spring, playing at full forward, had left the field injured in the second half and was replaced by Paddy 'Bawn' Brosnan. Just when it looked as if it was going to be a repeat of 1938, Charlie O'Sullivan, at left full forward, sent over Kerry's seventh and winning point with seconds remaining. It was a proud day for the Kingdom. They registered their fourteenth title in all and in so doing shared top place with Dublin.

Dublin took Kerry to a replay in the 1941 semi-final — a game the Kingdom won handsomely at Tralee — 2:9 to 0:3. Sunday, 7 September, saw a repeat of 1940, with Kerry, captained by Bill Dillon of Dingle, facing their now arch-rivals, Galway. It was their third meeting since 1938. With one victory each, 1941 would decide the rubber.

This was a thundering game of football between two very fit sides. The exchanges were teak tough. Strong, fit bodies tore into each other and mighty knocks were given and taken.

Galway had the better of the first half, but missed chances saw them only level at four points each at half-time. At the three-quarter stage, Tom O'Connor scored a smashing goal for Kerry to put them ahead by two points for the first time in the game. The score stood at 1:5 to 0:6. Kerry were now in the ascendancy and, with Dan O'Keeffe brilliant between the posts, they finished on the winning score of 1:8 to 0:7. Kerry were now the undisputed kings of football. With fifteen All-Ireland crowns, they headed the list.

Great names adorned that particular five-year era, among them Dan O'Keeffe, Joe Keohane, Bill Dillon, Eddie Walsh, Paddy Kennedy, Paddy 'Bawn' Brosnan, Murt Kelly, Johnny Walsh, Bill Casey, Tom O'Connor, Bill Myers, Seán Brosnan and Charlie O'Sullivan.

Returning to the men of more recent times and Kerry's successes between 1975 and 1986, in summary, Kerry's All-Ireland successes read as follows: 1975, when a young team won against the odds; four in a row from 1978 to 1981, with practically the same panel of players; three in a row from 1984 to 1986, with the bulk of the four-in-a-row players still participating (see the accompanying tables — pp 137–138).

The ability of so many of the players to perform with distinction in a variety of positions generated a synergy that gave a unique added value to the team and, on occasion, fashioned victory against the odds.

In that great era there were many memorable moments and personal achievements, such as the success of Paudie O'Shea — a man who abandoned the academic world to become a master of the football field. He conceded only one point from play to his opponents in eight finals. Denis 'Ogie' Moran played at centre forward in all eight winning finals — a record, and one that seems likely to stand for ever and a day.

In 1978, Mikey Sheehy scored a quick-thinking goal, against Paddy Cullen and Dublin, when he chipped an out-of-goal Paddy — one of football's most memorable and superb goals. Con Houlihan aptly likened the retreating Paddy to a woman who suddenly remembered that she had a cake in the oven — but too late. It would be hard to forget, either, the sheer football magic of Mikey as he performed acts of wizardry before scoring an 'impossible' goal against Cork in the dying seconds of the drawn Munster final of 1987.

There were two turning points in the game against Tyrone in 1986. Playing some grand football, Tyrone looked as if they would take their first title ever. Early in the second half they were awarded a penalty which, if converted, would have put them nine points ahead. Kerry's road back would have been difficult. Kevin McCabe pointed the penalty. Kerry breathed a sigh of relief. Later in that half, Pat Spillane ran onto the path of an incoming ball and, with the ingenuity of a master craftsman, deflected it with a two-fisted effort out of the reach of Tyrone goalkeeper and into the net.

Eight Texaco footballers-of-the-year awards were won by four Kerry players — John O'Keeffe (1975), Pat Spillane (1978 and 1986), Mikey Sheehy (1979), and Jack O'Shea (1980, 1981, 1984 and 1985).

Three players were chosen on the Centenary Football Team in 1984 — Jack O'Shea at midfield, Pat Spillane at left half-forward and Mikey Sheehy at right full forward.

The Kerry team of that era qualify for the title, 'best ever'. Shaped, moulded and inspired by coach Mick O'Dwyer, they extended the frontiers and widened the horizons of Gaelic football. Concentrating on total football, their sportsmanship was of the highest order. They were an example to youth and were great ambassadors for the game. They set standards that became a metaphor for greatness.

Their defenders were masterly, displaying at all times grace under pressure; their midfielders were supreme, raiding and punishing opposing defences; as for their forwards, we may never ever again see a combination to match the speed, precision, skill and class of Eoin Liston, Mikey Sheehy, John Egan, Pat Spillane, Denis 'Ogie' Moran and Ger Power — all of them swerving, weaving, dummying, mesmerising, side-stepping. They were all-conquering.

Le linn a ré bhí clú agus cáil agus iomrádh orthu. Is maith a thuileadar é. Ní raibh foireann in Éirinn incurtha leo agus ar ndóigh is dócha nach mbeidh riamh arís.

Kerry Players
Top Row: Páidí Ó Sé, Ogie Moran, Pat Spillane
Bottom Row: Ger Power, Michael Sheehy, Eoin Liston

KERRY defeated		1975 DUBLIN 2.12: 0.11	1978 DUBLIN 5.11: 0.9	1979 DUBLIN 3.13: 1.8	1980 ROSCOMMON 1.9: 1.6	1981 OFFALY 1.12: 0.8	1984 DUBLIN 0.14: 1.6	1985 DUBLIN 2.12: 2.8	1986 TYRONE 2.15: 1.10
Paudie O'Mahony	1	✓ ●	✓sub	–	–	–	–	–	–
Ger O'Keefe	2	✓	–	–	✓	✓sub	–	–	–
John O'Keefe	3	x ✓ ●	x ✓ ●	✓ ●	✓	x ✓	–	–	–
Jimmy Deenahan	4	x ✓	x ✓	✓	✓	x ✓c ●	–	–	–
Páidí Ó Sé	5	✓	x ✓	✓	✓	x ✓ ●	✓ ●	✓c ●	✓
Tim Kennelly	6	✓	x ✓	✓c ●	✓ ●	x ✓	–	–	–
Ger Power	7	x ✓ ●	x ✓ ●	subs' bench ●	✓c ●	x ✓	✓	✓	●
Paudie Lynch	8	✓	✓	✓	✓	✓	–	–	–
Pat McCarthy	9	✓	–	–	–	●	–	–	–
Brendan Lynch	10	x ✓	–	–	–	–	–	–	–
Denis 'Ogie' Moran	11	✓c ●	x ✓c	✓	✓	x ✓ ●	✓	✓	✓
Mickey O'Sullivan	12	✓ ●	–	–	–	–	–	–	–
John Egan	13	x ✓ ●	✓	✓	✓	x ✓	✓	–	–
Mikey Sheehy	14	✓	x ✓	✓ ●	✓	x ✓ ●	subs' bench ●	✓	✓ ●
Pat Spillane	15	✓	x ✓	✓ ●	✓ ●	x ✓sub ●	✓ ●	✓	✓ ●
Charlie Nelligan	16	–	✓	✓	✓ ●	x ✓	✓	✓	✓ ●
Ger O'Driscoll	17	✓sub	x –	–	✓sub	–	–	–	–
Mick Spillane	18	–	✓	✓	–	✓	✓	✓ ●	✓

KERRY defeated		1975 DUBLIN 2.12: 0.11	1978 DUBLIN 5.11: 0.9	1979 DUBLIN 3.13: 1.8	1980 ROSCOMMON 1.9: 1.6	1981 OFFALY 1.12: 0.8	1984 DUBLIN 0.14: 1.6	1985 DUBLIN 2.12: 2.8	1986 TYRONE 2.15: 1.10
Jack O'Shea	19	–	x	✓	✓ ●	x ✓ ●	✓ ●	✓ ●	✓
Sean Walsh	20	–	x	✓ ●	✓ ●	x ✓ ●	✓	✓	✓
Eoin Liston	21	–	✓	✓	subs' bench ●	x ●	✓ ●	✓	✓
Tommy Doyle	22	–	subs' bench	✓	✓	✓	✓ ●	✓ ●	✓c ●
Vincent O'Connor	23	–	–	✓sub	–	–	–	–	–
Tom Spillane	24	–	–	–	–	–	✓ ●	✓	✓ ●
Ger Lynch	25	–	–	–	–	–	✓	✓	✓
Ambrose O'Donovan	26	–	–	–	–	–	✓c	✓	✓
John Kennedy	27	–	–	–	–	–	✓	✓sub	–
Jimmy O'Dowd	28	–	–	–	–	–	✓sub	✓	✓sub
Willie Maher	29	–	–	–	–	–	–	–	✓

Twelve played in all four-in-a-row finals

Three played in all eight finals

● — All Star

c — captain

sub — came on as a substitute during the match

subs' bench — part of panel of substitutes

X — Played on winning Railway Cup team

X̲ — Came on as substitute for winning Railway Cup team

THE ALL-IRELAND FOOTBALL FINAL DRAWS

1894
Dublin (Young Irelands) v Cork (Nils)

The first and only draw in an All-Ireland final during the past century was in 1894. Very few teams competed in the championship that year and none whatsoever entered from either Connaught or Ulster.

In the Munster semi-final, Kerry beat Tipperary, but a replay was ordered by Central Council. Kerry refused to play and Tipperary were awarded the match. They then went on to meet Cork (Nils) in the final but were beaten.

In Leinster, Dublin (Young Irelands) and Meath (Navan Mahonys) met in the final, having beaten Wexford (Young Irelands) and Kilkenny respectively. However, it took three meetings before Dublin eventually triumphed, and became Leinster title holders in December.

The final was played on 24 March 1895 at Clonturk Park — the same day as the hurling final — and the referee was R.T. Blake of Meath. Dublin were captained by John Kennedy and the Cork's skipper was J. Leavy. The result was a draw, Cork 1:1; Dublin 0:6 (in those days one goal equalled five points).

The referee had exercised his discretion to play thirty minutes' extra time. However, Cork refused to play and Dublin were awarded the match. The Central Council then ordered a replay. This took place at Thurles on 21 April 1895 before a crowd of 10,000 spectators, which included Most Reverend Dr Croke. Again R.T. Blake refereed the game.

With only minutes remaining, the scoreboard read Cork 1:2; Dublin 0:5 (Cork two points ahead). Then Dublin refused to continue play because of pitch invasion and roughness from the sidelines. The referee gave no decision regarding the game, and did not declare either side as winners. No doubt, he remembered the drawn game and had learned therefrom.

Again, Central Council ordered a replay. Cork disagreed and withdrew from the Association for over twelve months in protest. The Cork County Board presented them with medals as All-Ireland Champions of 1894. However, Central Council awarded the game to Dublin and they became the official champions.

It was Dublin's third All-Ireland title. They had previously won in 1892 when they beat Laune Rangers of Kerry, 1:4 to 0:3. Their first win in 1891 was an interesting one. Dublin (Young Irelands) had taken three scores — 2 goals and 1 point — against Cork (Clondrohid) who had in turn taken ten scores — 1 goal and 9 points against Dublin. Nowadays, that would mean a Cork victory, 12 points to 7, but in 1891, no number of points matched a goal, with the result that Dublin's superior goal scoring carried the day.

1914

Kerry v Wexford

Kerry, who had accounted for Tipperary after an initial draw, defeated Cork in the Munster final by 5 points to 1, in Tralee on 4 October 1914.

Wexford had won the Leinster title when, on 18 August, before a large crowd, they got the better of Louth with a final score of 3 points to 1. Prior to that, they had accounted for Meath, Kilkenny and Dublin.

In the final, Kerry, captained by Dick Fitzgerald, faced Wexford, captained by Sean O'Kennedy, at Croke Park on 1 November 1914.

Twenty-six special trains travelled to Dublin for the game and a huge crowd — estimated at 15,000 — attended despite gloomy weather. 'Sliabh Ruadh' reported as follows:

> It was a great, close game, in which all the best elements of Gaelic football were served up in abundance. It was one of the greatest displays of science, speed and endurance yet witnessed under the Gaelic code. Both teams were trained to the hour and the ounce and a superb display was served up. It was the general opinion that Kerry were lucky to draw. Half-time scores: Wexford, 2 goals; Kerry, 1 point. Mr Harry Boland was referee.

> Final scores:- Wexford, 2 goals; Kerry, 1:3

Four weeks later the replay took place before a gathering of 20,000 fans. 'Sliabh Ruadh' wrote:

The game was well contested and Wexford made a bold bid for the title, leading at half-time by 6 points to nil. The typical dash of the Kerry men, however, pulled them through in the second half and the final scores were: Kerry, 2:3; Wexford, 6 points. Mr. Harry Boland was again referee. Kerry had two changes from the previous drawn game, bringing on Maurice McCarthy and Jack Rice.

'Vigilant' made the following comment: 'It was even a harder game than the one that ended in a drawn battle. It was fast, scientific and very clever all the way through, and fought out in an admirable sporting spirit.'

It was Kerry's fifth title.

1926

Kerry v Kildare

In 1926, Kerry defeated Tipperary in the Munster final by 11 points to 1:4, to take their fourth of five successive triumphs in the Munster Provincial championship.

Meanwhile in Connaught, Galway took the title for the province with two goals to spare over Mayo — 3:2 to 1:2.

Up North, Cavan had a decisive win over Antrim to take the Ulster title on the score 5:3 to 0:6.

In Leinster, Kildare emerged after an absence of seven years with a 6-point win over Wexford.

Then in the semi-finals, Kerry and Kildare had convincing wins over both Cavan and Galway respectively.

So Kerry, led by their captain, John Joe Sheehy, faced Kildare, skippered by Joe Loughlin, in what promised to be an intriguing and classic encounter. Classic it certainly turned out to be, in both the draw and the replay, matching

Larry Stanley (left) and Paddy Buggy

the excitement of the three games of the 1903 home final. (Details on the 1926 final are dealt with in the chapter entitled '1926: A Defining Moment' — pp 50–55.)

For Kerry, however, victory was tinged with sadness. Their outstanding defender and star of the drawn game, Jack Murphy, fell ill after that match and died before the replay.

Great players enhanced the occasion as the team line-outs for the replay demonstrate:

Kerry

Johnny Riordan (goal), P. Clifford, Joe Barrett, Jack Walsh, Paul Russell, J. Moriarty, John Slattery, Con Brosnan, Bob Stack, John Ryan, Des O'Connell, Tom Mahoney, Jas Bailey, Bill Gorman, John Joe Sheehy (Captain)

Kildare

James Cummins (goal), Michael Buckley, Matt Goff, B. Graham, Frank Malone, Jack Higgins, John Hayes, P. Martin, Gus Fitzpatrick, Larry Stanley, Paul Doyle, T. Donoghue, Joe Curtis, William Gannon, Joe Loughlin (Captain)

1937

Kerry *v* Cavan

In 1937, Kerry appeared in their first final since their great four-in-a-row wins of 1929–1932.

On this occasion, their opponents were Cavan and, strangely enough, it was the first time that these two counties had met in an All-Ireland final.

Kerry were captained by Mick Doyle, and Cavan were skippered by Tom O'Reilly.

Both counties had had easy provincial victories — Kerry had defeated Clare with seventeen points to spare, winning 4:9 to 1:1, and Cavan had beaten Armagh by 13 points to 3.

In the first semi-final on 15 August, Kerry were fortunate to draw with a very gallant Laois outfit, 2:3 to 1:6. Two weeks later, at the replay, they were equally fortunate to survive by one point, taking victory by 2:2 to 1:4.

Similarly, in the second semi-final, on 22 August, Cavan survived a great Mayo challenge and earned their place in the final by just one point.

The 1937 title was not going to be won easily. At Croke Park, on 26 September, Cavan held Kerry to a draw — 2:5 to 1:8 — in a thrilling game of high-standard football. The replay took place on 17 October and this time Kerry found gaps in the Cavan defence, scoring four goals and as many points to Cavan's total of 1:7. So it was that Kerry took their twelfth All-Ireland football title in a game which, sadly, hadn't lived up to the standard of the drawn encounter.

1938
Galway v Kerry

The year of 1938 was unusual as it was the first time ever that All-Ireland finals were drawn in two successive years.

It was also unique in that, for the second consecutive year in the semi-finals, the Munster champions played the Leinster champions and the Connaught title holders played the Ulster winners.

The latter-stage games produced the following results:

Kerry 4:14; Clare 0:6 — Munster final

Kerry 2:6; Laois 2:4 — All-Ireland semi-final

Galway 0:8; Mayo 0:5 — Connaught final

Galway 2:10; Monaghan 2:3 — All-Ireland semi-final

The scene was now set for a great Kerry v Galway showdown in the final. Again, it was a novel pairing with tradition favouring a Kerry victory.

Galway, playing fine football, and showing scant regard for tradition, held the Kerrymen to a draw in one of the finest exhibitions of the code ever witnessed in Croke Park. The game which took place before a record attendance of 68,950 people had a strange ending though. With the seconds ticking away and the scores level, Kerry were awarded a 'fifty'. It was taken by John Joe 'Purty' Landers and, while the ball was in flight, but before it went over for a point, the referee blew the final whistle.

The replay had an even more amazing finish. The referee blew the whistle for a free with about two minutes remaining. The crowd took it to be the final whistle and rushed onto the pitch, the Galway fans cheering their heroes who were leading by four points. By the time order was restored, following an announcement over the loud speaker, several of the Kerry players had left the ground, believing that the game was over. All available subs were called upon to finish the game but it isn't clear whether or not Kerry were able to muster together a full fifteen. In the end, Galway won, 2:4 to 0:7 — their third All-Ireland crown.

Martin Kelly played right full-forward on that Galway team. He spent many years as a Garda in my native parish of Ardagh in West Limerick. Tall, rangy and well built, he was a most affable and amiable gentleman. I was too young at the time to discuss the All-Ireland details with him, but I did know that he was proud of his All-Ireland medal, and doubly proud that it was won at the expense of Kerry, from whence his wife, Nora, came.

Every Galwayman was a hero — J. McGauran had kept a clean goal; at full back and centre back Mick Connaire and Bobby Beggs had been brilliant, as had been the other defenders, Mick Raftery, Dinny O'Sullivan, Frank Cunniffe and Charlie Connolly; John Dunne and John Burke had held the midfield, while the forwards, J. Flavin, Ramie Griffin, Mick Higgins, Ned Mulholland, Martin Kelly and Brendan Nestor, who had not seen as much of the ball as their Kerry counterparts, had been more opportunistic, and this factor had carried the day for Galway.

1943

Roscommon v Cavan

The year of 1943 saw the rise to prominence of a great Roscommon team. They hadn't won the Connaught title since 1914 and were now building on the successes of their minors — All-Ireland champions in 1939 and 1941 — and their juniors — All-Ireland champions in 1940.

In 1941 and 1942 Roscommon had failed to Galway by only one point in the Connaught final.

By 1943, a new set of great football names was coming to the fore. They would be prominent throughout the 1940s — they were Bill Jackson, Brendan Lynch, Bill Carlos, Owensie Hoare, Eddie Boland, Liam Gilmartin, Phelim Murray, Jimmy Murray, Donal Keenan, Jack McQuillan, Frankie Kinlough, John Joe

Nerney, John Joe Fallon and Mick Culhane among others. Many of them rank with the immortals of the game.

In 1943, they emerged from Connaught with a four-point win over Galway, and then beat Louth by a similar margin in the All-Ireland semi-final.

Their opponents, Cavan, had beaten Monaghan in the Ulster final — also with four points to spare. It was closer for Cavan against Cork in the semi-final, with just one point separating the teams at full time.

The drawn All-Ireland final of 1943 — another unique final pairing, with Cavan in search of a third title and Roscommon seeking a first — drew a crowd of 68,000. It was generally felt that Roscommon were somewhat unfortunate not to have won.

On 10 October, Roscommon faced a replay before a much smaller crowd of just over 47,000 — no doubt the prevailing war-time conditions were responsible for the lower attendance.

The game turned out to be a tough, physical encounter with a lot of heavy charging. Cavan lost their full forward Joe Stafford early in the second half when he was sent to the sideline following an altercation with Roscommon half-back, Owensie Hoare.

The game had reached injury time when Cavan players attempted to stop the umpire waving the white flag for a Roscommon point which brought the score to 2:7 to 2:2 against Cavan.

When a Cavan player assaulted the referee, Paddy Mythen of Wexford, and he fell to the ground, some of the crowd invaded the pitch. The game was restarted but the referee blew full time. He was again attacked by a Cavan player and jostled by some spectators before being escorted to the dressing-room by gardaí and officials.

Nothing, however, could overshadow Roscommon's historic victory and there was jubilation when GAA President Seamus Gardiner presented the Sam Maguire Cup to Roscommon Captain Jimmy Murray, who had played brilliantly in both games.

A year later, Roscommon added to their prestige when they trounced Cavan in the semi-final by 17 points. They then went on to beat mighty Kerry in the final by 2 points before a record attendance of 79,000 people.

No wonder Roscommon fans danced in the street that night as they celebrated a famous victory.

1946

Kerry v Roscommon

Oh the month it was October and '46 the year,
When Kerry and Roscommon clashed to make the verdict clear.
Roscommon's captain bragged before the glorious game began,
Today we'll beat the Kingdom sweet for horse or hound or man.

In the championships of 1946, Kerry romped through the Munster final with a 2:16 to 2:1 win over Waterford, and so replaced All-Ireland champions, Cork, as Munster title holders.

In Leinster, Laois had a two-point win over Kildare 0:11 to 1:6, and took the provincial title, for the first time since 1938 when they had concluded a great three-in-a-row series of wins in the province.

In Ulster, Antrim, a team with some really outstanding footballers, proved to be a surprise package. They had displayed superb combination, coupled with quickly executed hand-passing forward movements, to defeat Cavan (kingpins of Ulster football for over a quarter century) in the provincial final.

In the west, Roscommon had emerged victorious again, having survived a Mayo objection. They had won the final by 1:4 to 0:6 against Mayo, but following the objection a replay was ordered.

On the second time out, there was no doubt about the superior team, Roscommon winning by 1:9 to 1:2.

The scene was now set for two unique semi-final pairings that produced the following very close results — results, in both cases, where the losers might very well have been very worthy winners.

Kerry 2:7; Antrim 0:10, — 18 August at Croke Park

Roscommon 3:5; Laois 2:6 — 25 August at Croke Park

In 1946, other factors outside football came into play, which and it is important to outline them. From the middle of the year downpours of rain had made 1946 the wettest year in living memory; and as the year progressed fears grew for the harvest.

The Second World War had ended in 1945 and, by the summer of 1946, private cars — not that there were many of them — were back on the roads again. Transport in general had begun to improve.

As the rain continued and the outlook worsened for the country's crops, the Government called for volunteers from all walks of life to assist in saving the harvest. To this end the All-Ireland football final was postponed and did not take place until 6 October that year.

I can still remember Mícheál O'Hehir describing the closing five minutes of the 1946 final as the 'impossible' unfolded and the excitement became intense. For fifty-five minutes Roscommon held Kerry to four points and led by 1:7 to 0:4. They looked certain to win. The Roscommon captain, Jimmy Murray, was on the sideline being attended to for a severe nose injury — he looked quite a mess. The St John's ambulance man said to him, as he cleaned away the blood, 'I want to make you presentable to receive the cup,' it seemed a foregone conclusion at that time.

Then came a goal for Kerry from full forward, 'lovely dark-haired Paddy Burke'. It was in such circumstances, that Mícheál O'Hehir used say, 'The game isn't over yet', and 'Can Kerry now pull the game out of the fire?' Time was ticking away. My own recollection of those dying seconds is that Kerry's second sensational and equalising goal by Tom 'Gega' O'Connor came from a sideline ball.

Roscommon supporters, amongst an attendance of almost 76,000, were stunned and bewildered, while elated Kerry fans looked forward to the replay.

This took place on 27 October. Kerry's captain in the drawn game, Gus Cremins, was now among the subs. Consequently, Paddy Kennedy of Annascaul was moved from centre forward to centre field and given the captaincy. This time the game was close all the way through, and as the end approached, the scores were level. Then Gus Cremins was brought into the game. He fielded a Roscommon clearance around midfield and sent it soaring over the bar to take the lead for Kerry. A Kerry goal followed, which in turn was followed by the final whistle; Kerry were All-Ireland champions for the sixteenth time.

1952

Cavan *v* Meath

In 1952, Meath were the only senior football team to retain their provincial crown, taking a 1-point win over Louth.

Roscommon defeated All-Ireland champions, Mayo, to regain the Connaught title after a lapse of five years. Meanwhile, Cavan re-established themselves in Ulster with one goal to spare over Monaghan and thus replaced Antrim as the title holders.

Down south, Cork, for once, had it easy over reigning provincial champions, Kerry, as the score of the final testifies: 11 points to 2.

The semi-final games resulted as follows:

Meath 1:6; Roscommon 0:7 — 3 August at Croke Park

Cavan 0:10; Cork 2:3 — 17 August at Croke Park

The meeting of Cavan and Meath in the final was a repeat of the 1949 final, except that this time the result was reversed.

In 1952, Cavan had only three survivors from their historic win over Kerry in the All-Ireland final, played in New York, in 1947 — Tony Tighe, Edwin Carolan and their captain, New-York-born Mick Higgins. Mick, still playing at centre forward, had been awarded Man of the Year for his leadership qualities and his accuracy from placed balls.

Despite strong winds and very heavy rain, both teams served up exciting and entertaining fare, with Edwin Carolan scoring the equalising point for Cavan on the call of time.

Rain again marred the replay on 12 October but there were still 60,000 spectators in attendance. The replay wasn't as good as the drawn game and, for the first time since 1927, neither side scored a goal. The match ended with the score of Cavan 0:9; Meath 0:5 — Cavan's fifth All-Ireland title and their last to date. This contest between the two neighbouring counties was close man-to-man football all the way through — no frills. Each player had got to know his opponent well during the drawn game. Scores were at a premium, and at half-time it was 3 points to 2 in Cavan's favour. Seven of Cavan's nine points came from the unerring boot of Mick Higgins — all from frees — despite the greasy ball and slippery pitch. An interesting feature of the game was the fact that members of the same family played on opposite sides. B. Maguire was centre field for Meath while his brothers, Dessie and Liam, played at left full back and centre back respectively, for Cavan.

1972

Offaly v Kerry

In 1972, Kerry avenged their 11-point Munster-final defeat by Cork, the previous year, with a 6-point victory, 2:21 to 2:15.

Meanwhile, Roscommon, after a decade in the wilderness, took the Connaught title with four points to spare over Mayo.

Donegal celebrated in Ulster and, for the first time in their history, were crowned senior football champions of the province after their win over Tyrone by 2:13 to 1:11.

Offaly, who had won their first All-Ireland senior football title in 1971, retained their Leinster title in 1972 with a good win over Kildare — 1:18 to 2:8. They were the only team to retain their provincial crown that year.

The results of the 1972 semi-finals were as follows:

Kerry 1:22; Roscommon 1:12 — 13 August at Croke Park

Offaly 1:17; Donegal 2:10 — 20 August at Croke Park

The final was contested by Offaly and Kerry, the second meeting of the two counties at that level. Kerry had previously triumphed over Offaly in 1969, 10 points to 7. An intriguing contest was in prospect, and so it proved to be, the teams all square at the end with 1:13 apiece. Yet again, the destiny of the Sam Maguire Cup had to await the outcome of a replay. The question on all lips was whether Offaly could retain their title and take 'Sam' back to the 'Faithful' county for the second time in the history of the game; or whether Kerry's record, tradition and performance in replays, would prove to be a trump card. Only time would tell.

Of the eight All-Ireland replays up to that date, Kerry had taken part in five and lost only once — to Galway in 1938.

The 1972 replay took place on 15 October before a crowd of over 66,000 spectators. It put the standard of the previously drawn game in the shade. Playing against a strong wind and into the railway goal, Offaly were on level terms at half-time — the score standing at 8 points each. In the second half, Offaly turned on the style and the splendour. They had both speed and stamina in abundance, and heroic players too — in fact, all were heroes, but some were particularly excellent. Martin Furlong, in goal, was brilliant — his anticipation uncanny. Mick Ryan, at right full back, was superb in a great full back line that included Paddy McCormack and Larry Coughlan. At midfield, Willie Bryan was majestic in everything he did, and in the forward line, Tony McTague, their captain and deadly accurate free taker, had 10 points to his credit.

In a Kerry team that was outclassed in the second half, only Donie O'Sullivan at right full back and Mick O'Connell at midfield, stood apart.

The scoreboard at the final whistle left Kerry supporters bewildered — Offaly 1:19; Kerry 0:13. It was Kerry's biggest defeat in an All-Ireland final. 'Sam' returned to Offaly and so did their team of heroes as listed hereunder:

Martin Furlong
Mick Ryan, Paddy McCormack, Larry Coughlan
Eugene Mulligan, Sean Lowry, Martin Heavey
Sean Evans, Willie Bryan
Johnny Cooney, Kevin Kilmurray, Tony McTague
Seamus Darby, John Smith, Paddy Fenning
Playing Subs: Murt Connor, Nicholas Clavin, Mick Wright
who each replaced Johnny Cooney, Eugene Mulligan and Larry
Coughlan, respectively

1988

Meath v Cork

In 1988, Cork were becoming the dominant football power in Munster and were slowly getting the measure of their arch rivals, Kerry.

The county with the most dominant team in Connaught alternated, mainly between Mayo, Galway and Roscommon, but in 1988, Mayo were supreme.

By 1988, the days of Cavan's prominence in Ulster belonged in the distant past. They had taken their last title in 1969 and since then Derry, Down, Donegal, Tyrone and Armagh had also shared the successes. So too had Monaghan, who in 1988 emerged to capture a third Ulster crown, their thirteenth in all.

Meath and Dublin were dominating Leinster and, in 1988, Meath completed a hat trick of victories over Dublin with a win of 2:5 to 0:9.

The semi-finals of 1988 produced decisive results but from disappointing games.

Cork 1:14; Monaghan 0:6 — 14 August at Croke Park

Meath 0:16; Mayo 2:5 — 21 August at Croke Park

The final, between Meath — reigning All-Ireland and National League champions — and Cork, was a repeat of the 1987 final. In 1988, however, Meath were in search of their second in a row, and a fifth All-Ireland title.

Cork too were seeking a fifth title and their first since 1973.

Fortune favoured Meath in a drawn game that ended on the score Cork 1:9; Meath 0:12, after what had been a tough, physical, hard-hitting match. The replay would be the third meeting of these teams in an All-Ireland final within thirteen months.

A tense encounter was in prospect, but no one could have foreseen the drama that unfolded in the early moments. With a little over five minutes gone, Gerry McEntee, who formed a brilliant midfield partnership with Liam Hayes for Meath, was sent off.

Meath were now really up against it and had to dig deep into their reserves of mental and physical energy. But dig deep they did. They chased and harassed the Cork players while maintaining good support for each other. They successfully withstood long spells of Cork dominance and were a point to the good at the final whistle, 13 points to 12.

Physically, it was a gruelling game and tensions ran high on the pitch — and they ran high afterwards too. Cork would look back and ponder over the fact that an old failing, of not being able to convert possession and superiority into scores, certainly cost them the game. Still, nothing could take away from the determination, tenacity and verve of the Meathmen.

Joe Cassells, a veteran aged 34 who had been nursing injuries, had been recalled to the centre forward position for the replay.

It was his first game of the 1988 championship and the captaincy was transferred to him from Mick Lyons. Joe became the first captain to receive the new Sam Maguire Cup and he returned in triumph to a huge welcome in Royal Meath.

1996

Meath *v* Mayo

When Meath and Mayo lined out for the All-Ireland football final of 1996 it was only the second such encounter between these two counties.

They had first met in an All-Ireland final in 1951 when Mayo were captained by Sean Flanagan and Meath were captained by Seamus Heery. At the semi-final stage of that year's championship, Meath had defeated Antrim 2:6 to 1:7, while Mayo, after a draw with Kerry, had won the semi-final replay by 2:4 to 1:5. Mayo completed a successful year by defeating Meath in the final 2:8 to 0:9. The victory made it two in a row and three titles in all for them.

Denis Daly, recounting that win in the *Western People*, on 2 October 1996, noted that, in 1951, 'there was electricity rationing, you could buy a Ford Anglia car for £372, a tweed overcoat for £8 and you could get a job with Bord na Mona at rates of up to 2/- per hour'.

In between those years, Mayo won eight Connaught titles, but succeeded in reaching the final only once; that was in 1989 when they lost to Cork.

Meath fared better. They won eleven Leinster titles, contested nine All-Ireland finals and were victorious on four occasions, the most recent of which were two in a row in 1987 and 1988.

However, all of that was mere history when referee Pat McEnaney of Monaghan threw the ball in for the start of the final of 1996 — Meath in search of a sixth title and Mayo seeking a fourth.

There was a definite contrast in styles: Mayo favoured a passing game that consumed a lot of energy, while Meath played more direct football. The key question was, who would make the best use of their opportunities by avoiding squander-mania and translating possession into scores?

Time and again, Mayo swept down the field like a well-drilled military unit, but they failed to penetrate the Meath fortress. Meath fell back and covered and tackled, and the net result? Wasted hard-won Mayo possession.

Meath never led during the entire match but they were level from the fourteenth to the seventeenth minute. Mayo dominated and controlled, and comprehensively out-played Meath for most of the seventy minutes; all the while looking the far superior team. Victory seemed assured as they led by 6 points ten minutes into the second half. However, if the referee had chosen to play extra time, Meath might well have stolen victory, for they rallied in the closing fifteen minutes.

Tom Humphries, writing in *The Irish Times* summed it up well:

> *The minutes slipped by. Three points ahead and Mayo were losing shape. Two points ahead and Mayo were losing confidence. One point ahead and Mayo were losing their faith. Level and the final whistle was greeted like a hangman's reprieve.*

There was an eerie silence in Croke Park.

Jim Sullivan in *The Examiner* had this to say:

> *For all but the closing five minutes Mayo remained strongly in contention with powerful covering in defence, marvellous play from McHale and aggressive forward play. Their Achilles heel was that they regularly wasted possession.*

In the *Irish Sun*, Peadar O'Brien wrote:

> *To Mayo I say — you had the winning of this game in the first half. You didn't take it. To Meath I say — You can thank experience for this great escape.*

Meath's equaliser, on the call of time, resembled a plot from a Hitchcock thriller. Staunch Meath half-back Colm Coyle let fly a mighty kick from 70 yards. It hopped on the hard ground in front of goal as two backs and two forwards jostled for possession. The Mayo goalkeeper, John Madden, could only look on in dismay as the ball bounced high over the crossbar.

It was little consolation to Mayo that Liam McHale got the Man-of-the-Match Award.

The replay was held two weeks later on Sunday, 29 September 1996. After only six minutes of play, the 'father and mother' of all fracas erupted at the railway end of the pitch and the bulk of both teams became involved. When calm was restored, Liam McHale and Colm Coyle received marching orders from the referee. To this day, people say, 'Why just those two?'

Here are some comments on the game:

Truly the best team came second at Croke Park yesterday. Had the Connaught champions won by six points it would have been justified. Had Eoin 'Bomber' Liston been at full forward, it would have been twelve and therein lies the tale of the replay. (Larry Tompkins, The Examiner*)*

Again the better team in yesterday's fiery replay in Croke Park, gallant Mayo, experienced the unforgiving nature of sport. Sean Boylan's team were the men to triumph for the simple reason that they were more adept at taking their chances. (Jim Sullivan, The Examiner*)*

The scoreboard never lies. Meath are champions. Mayo players fell to the ground, spent after their exhaustive feats. Spent. Desolate. And unrewarded. The scoreboard can be harsh. (Liam Horan, Irish Independent*)*

Yes indeed, the scoreboard can be harsh; but in any game, when the final whistle blows, the only superiority that counts is that which is reflected on the scoreboard. All others — such as style, speed, finesse, possession, dominance and skill — become secondary.

Mayo led for sixty minutes of the match; then a goal put Meath ahead, but five minutes later Mayo drew level with a point. However, on the call of time, a point scored by Brendan O'Reilly sealed the victory for Meath. The Sam Maguire Cup was on the way, in the words of Padraic Colum, 'To Meath of the pastures'.

Results of the 1996 All-Ireland Football Final

First Match: Meath 0:12; Mayo 1:9

Replay: Meath 2:9; Mayo 1:11

L–R
all Kerry
P. Burke
P. Kennedy
G. Cremins

L–R
M. Higgin (Cavan)
M. Furlong (Offaly)
T. O'Reilly (Cavan)

L–R
all Roscommon
B. Lynch
B. Jackson
J. Murray

L–R
all Roscommon
J. McQuillan
E. Boland
W. Carlos

L–R
all Roscommon
P. Murray
D. Keenan
F. Kinlough

L–R
all Roscommon
J.J. Fallon
M. Culhane

A selection of players from the Kerry, Cavan, Offaly and Roscommon teams.

THE GOAL-LESS ALL-IRELAND HURLING TRIUMPHS

At the time of writing this book, there have been only three occasions in the history of the GAA when the winners of the All-Ireland senior hurling title have failed to score a goal. These are as follows:

1947	Kilkenny 0:14; Cork 2:7 (13)
1961	Tipperary 0:16; Dublin 1:12 (15)
1997	Clare 0:20; Tipperary 2:13 (19)

It is also interesting to note that the winners on each occasion had only one point to spare when the final whistle sounded.

1947: Kilkenny *v* Cork

I lost 6 shillings (30 pence) to Willie O'Connell, Assistant Manager at the local Creamery in Ardagh, on this occasion. The previous year, I had placed a similar bet with Willie on the winners, Cork, and felt rich when I collected my winnings. He was reluctant to dispossess me in 1947 but I insisted and then went off wondering about my judgement. I had been reading all the previews and I knew that Kilkenny had improved on the previous year. At the same time, Cork looked very solid on paper. I also felt that Kilkenny had used up all their luck in the semi-final against Galway at Birr. As well as that, they were in search of a thirteenth title — unlucky, I felt.

Apart from the game at Birr, Kilkenny cruised into the All-Ireland final with the following victories:

v *Wexford at Nowlan Park, 5:11 to 3:8*
v *Dublin at Portlaoise, 7:10 to 3:8*
v *Galway at Birr, 2:9 to 1:11*

The game at Birr was thrilling and was won in 'lost time', thanks to Terry Leahy and Jimmy Langton. However, it was a day when a draw would have been a fairer result.

Cork's passage to the final was somewhat similar, apart from their clash with Limerick.

v *Clare, 4:9 to 0:4*

v *Waterford at Clonmel, 3:10 to 1:5*

v *Limerick at Thurles, 2:6 to 2:3*

v *Antrim at Croke Park, 7:10 to 0:5*

Cork were fortunate to escape with a win at Thurles and, on reflection, maybe they had used up all their luck on that occasion (as I thought Kilkenny had against Galway). A press report on the game said: 'If ever a better team lost it was Limerick ... they were magnificent in as dour a Southern decider as was ever played ... a richly deserved victory was denied....' Between this match and Kilkenny's game at Birr, it could very well have been a Galway *v* Limerick final in 1947.

The day of the final itself had begun with a heavy morning's rain. However, the gloom had been replaced with blue skies by the time that referee Phil Purcell — a sterling Tipperary defender of earlier years — got the game under way. A crowd of 61,510 spectators had gathered to see the action that day.

Kilkenny, playing against the breeze in the first half, showed their class from early on. All of their lines were solid and goalkeeper Jim Donegan was brilliant throughout the hour. Kilkenny kept picking off their points while Cork, unwisely, were trying for goals. As a result, Cork missed out on several points which were there for the taking. At the break, in this free-flowing, fast and entertaining game, Kilkenny led by 0:7 to 0:5 — no goals to either side. Jim Langton had scored 3 points for Kilkenny while Tom Walton, Jack Mulcahy, Shem Downey and Terry Leahy had taken one apiece.

The scorers for Cork were: Sean Condon, 3 points, with Joe Kelly and Jack Lynch scoring one each. Centre forward Christy Ring (profiled in *Giants of the Ash* and *Hurling*) was being contained by Peter Prendergast — and thereby hangs a tale. Peter seemed to be glued to Ring and even Kilkenny folk felt that a less indulgent referee might well have seen Kilkenny pay the penalty.

As the game entered its final phase, the score stood at 0:9 to 0:7 in Kilkenny's favour. From then until the end of the match, all the drama and pandemonium of one hundred battles unfolded. Mossie O'Riordan found the net for Cork and this put them ahead for the first time. Immediately, Tom Walton equalised with a point for Kilkenny, making the score 0:10 to 1:7. A rampant Terry Leahy sent two more over the bar to score for Kilkenny, and their supporters went wild. Lost time was being played — there were over six minutes of it in all — when Joe Kelly scored what looked like being the winning goal for Cork. Their supporters were in ecstasy as Cork took the lead on the score of 2:7 to 0:12.

Shortly after the puck-out, a free was awarded to Kilkenny. From a very tight angle, some thirty yards out from the Cork goal, Terry Leahy — 'Mr Cool' (who was later to be known as 'Mr Hurling', in America) stepped up to take the free. 'I wouldn't be in his boots for all the tea in China,' said Commentator Mícheál O'Hehir, as Terry stooped, then lifted and struck the sliotar to take the equaliser for Kilkenny. Everyone in Croke Park was agog, convinced that time was up and that the result was a draw. The referee looked at his watch but play continued. A Cork attack was repulsed by Paddy Grace and Kilkenny countered by storming in on the Cork goal. Tom Mulcahy's clearance to Hill 16 was anticipated by Terry Leahy who then took possession. As he prepared to strike, he turned to Alan Lotty and said, 'This is it, Alan', and he was absolutely right. The winner sailed over the crossbar — Terry Leahy's sixth point of the day. Then it was all over. The final score was: Kilkenny 0:14; Cork 2:7.

It was Kilkenny's thirteenth All-Ireland title but it had taken magic — the magic of Terry Leahy — to win it. They had failed in 1940, 1945 and 1946, and in the closing minutes of the 1947 final, it was almost as though they were at battle with the gods. Twice during the game it seemed that the title had been whipped irretrievably from their grasp.

However, Kilkenny's approach and tactics had all paid dividends. Their shooting accuracy, policy of going for points, refusal to panic and seek goals in the dying moments, combined with their speed off the mark, their energy, and above all their hunger — ah yes, their hunger! — gave them the edge over Cork.

Terry Leahy

Since Kilkenny had had their last All-Ireland victory in 1939, they had lost to Limerick in 1940, Tipperary in 1945 and Cork in 1946. By comparison, Cork had won five titles in the period from 1939 to 1947.

The 1947 final had been a hurling epic and its climax was breathtaking. It was the first goalless victory in an All-Ireland final since the competition began, but from a Kilkenny point of view, it was oh, so sweet.

1947 All-Ireland Final
Kilkenny Line-out

Jim Donegan (Eoghan Ruadhs) Dublin

Paddy Grace (Dicksboro), Paddy Hayden (Éire Óg),
Mark Marnell (Tullaroan)

Jimmy Kelly (Carrickshock), Peter Prendergast (Tullaroan),
Jack Mulcahy (Éire Óg)

Jimmy Heffernan (Carrickshock), Dan Kennedy (Captain) (Thomastown)

Tom Walton Terry Leahy Jimmy Langton
(Tullaroan) (Faughs-Dublin) (Éire Óg)

Shem Downey (Tullaroan), Willie Cahill (Graigue),
Liam Reidy (Éire Óg)

1961
Tipperary v Dublin

In my mind, what stands out most about the 1961 final is Liam Devaney's performance for Tipperary after he was switched from centre forward position to centre back. This occurred late in the game, and at that stage Dublin were beginning to look as though they would take the title. However, the switch of Devaney's position proved to be a trump card for Tipperary. There was a dash and fire attached to his hurling, as well as a high degree of panache. He held the centre, cleared his lines and hurled with confidence, leaving no gaps for his opponents. Without a doubt, he was a key element in Tipperary's narrow win over Dublin.

Tipperary were the clear favourites in the final of 1961, despite the fact that they had lost the previous year's final to Wexford by 2:15 to 0:11, and that Dublin had beaten Wexford in the Leinster final 7:5 to 4:8. (This was not the first time that Dublin had proven to be Wexford's bogey team.)

Tipperary had a number of injury problems, and their biggest worry was Jimmy Doyle who had decided he was going to play, irrespective of medical advice. Jimmy wasn't going to miss lining out for his county in an All-Ireland final. In the Munster final against Cork, his ankle had been fractured in two places and medical opinion was very specific: he should not play, he was risking his leg. However, with the aid of pain-killing injections just before the game and again at half-time, risk it he did. His contribution to the Tipperary victory was enormous. Out of a team total of 16 points, Jimmy scored 9 of them, 2 from play and 7 from frees.

On an ideal day for hurling, 67,866 eager spectators watched as referee Gerry Fitzgerald of Limerick began the game. The first half of the match, while entertaining and enjoyable, was more like a friendly than an All-Ireland final. Dublin were very fit and used their speed to move the sliotar well. However, their share of possession was not reflected on the scoreboard. Tipperary led at half-time by 10 points to 6.

The second half was set alight after only five minutes' play when Billy Jackson found the net for Dublin. From then on the crowd was treated to splendid hurling and real All-Ireland excitement. Midway through the half, Achill Boothman levelled the score with a point for Dublin. Shortly after, when Lar Shannon gave Dublin a point lead, a surprise result seemed to be on the cards.

Des Foley was playing very well at midfield for Dublin and their full back line of Des Ferguson, Noel Drumgoole and Lar Foley was rock-solid. The Boothman brothers, Achill and Bernie, were moving well in attack. However, just when Dublin appeared to be getting the upper hand, they were dealt a hammer-blow. Their sterling defender, Lar Foley, was sent off, together with Tom Ryan of Tipperary. For Dublin, the loss was greater and it probably cost them the game. Strange as it may seem, I have no recollection of the incident myself. Perhaps I didn't see it happen, or else it has been erased from my memory. Either way, it must have been fairly serious or Gerry Fitzgerald, well known for his common sense and pragmatism, would not have dismissed them from the field.

When fate is unkind, it can be really unkind. Jimmy Gray, one of Dublin's great goalkeepers, can still see the wide 'point' that was flagged for Tipperary as he looked up to see the sliotar go well outside the uprights. His brother, who was stewarding and had an excellent view of the incident, was absolutely furious at the decision. This point was awarded in the last quarter of the match when Dublin were ahead and looking to consolidate their position. In addition, during the course of the hour, there were two dubious frees awarded against Des Ferguson for allegedly picking the ball off the ground; both incidents resulted in Tipperary's scoring points. However, apart from all that, Dublin had had their chances. Opportunities were missed that they would bemoan, and even right at the end there was a free which, if converted, would have drawn the game; but Dublin did not have a Jimmy Doyle.

Throughout the game though, Tipperary made fewer errors, took their chances and coped well with any adversities that they encountered. At one stage they even had to replace their centre back, Tony Wall, who retired injured.

The final whistle brought a thrilling second half to an end, with the score Tipperary 0:16; Dublin 1:12. Tipperary had won their eighteenth crown while Dublin had failed in their bid for a seventh. Matt Hassett, the captain of the winning side, proudly took the MacCarthy Cup back to Toomevara.

In the final of 1961, Donie Nealon earned his second All-Ireland medal, which was, of course, wonderful to win; but for Donie, the victory lacked an important ingredient — a goal, a green flag. When speaking to me during the time that I was writing *Legends of the Ash*, Donie expressed his feelings on this matter: 'Nothing lifts a match like goals — the green flag waving. I think it's a sign of a defect not to get a goal. When we beat Dublin in 1961 by 0:16 to 1:12, I felt the victory was a little bit hollow. We never shook the net.' Still, a victory is a victory — even if it is a goal-less one.

1961 All-Ireland Final

Tipperary Line-out

Donal O'Brien (Knockavilla-Kickhams)

Matt Hassett (Toomevara), Michael Maher (Thurles Sarsfields)
Kieran Carey (Roscrea)

Mick Burns (Éire Óg — Nenagh), Tony Wall (Thurles Sarsfields)
John Doyle (Holycross)

Theo English (Marlfield), Matt O'Gara (Toomevara)

Jimmy Doyle (Thurles Sarsfields), Liam Devaney (Borrisoleigh)
Donie Nealon (Burgess)

John McKenna (Borrisokane), Billy Muloughney (Killadangan)
Tom Muloughney (Kilruane-McDonagh)

1997

Clare v Tipperary

Hurling folk in County Clare will never forget the All-Ireland final, of 1997. For years to come, they will watch the video over and over again and relish every moment of the game. They will also relive the agony and the ecstasy of those last ten minutes when fortunes swayed, hearts missed a beat and drama upon drama brought tension to bursting point.

Even before the sliotar was thrown in, this one-hundred and tenth final had become historic. For the first time, two Munster teams were meeting in an All-Ireland final. This had been brought about by the decision to allow the defeated finalists of Munster and Leinster back into the championship. (This had been done with a view to providing more games for the championship that year, generating more finance and promoting the game in general.)

Clare and Tipperary each had four matches to play on their different roads to Croke Park for the All-Ireland hurling final that year.

Clare won all of their game, with the following results:

v *Kerry 3:24 to 1:6*

v *Cork 1:19 to 0:18*

v *Tipperary 1:18 to 0:18*

v *Kilkenny 1:17 to 1:13*

Clare were carrying the scalps of the 'big three', any of which were capable of winning the All-Ireland. The 1997 final would be their fifth and they were seeking their third championship title.

Tipperary won three of their qualifying matches, losing only to Clare. The results are as follows:

v *Limerick 1:20 to 0:13*

v *Clare 0:18 to 1:18*

v *Down 3:24 to 3:8*

v *Wexford 2:16 to 0:15*

Tipperary were carrying the scalps of both finalists of the previous year, Limerick and Wexford — good credentials indeed. The 1997 All-Ireland final would be their thirty-third and they were in search of their twenty-fifth title. There was a lot of pride at stake and it was the first time Clare had beaten them in a Munster final. There was much to play for in the final and Croke Park was a mass of blue and gold as the teams marched in the pre-match parade. Both counties have the same colours and only the jersey design differed, with Clare having perhaps a slightly lighter hue.

There was an air of excitement and expectation as the crowd eagerly awaited the throw-in, following the playing and singing of 'Amhrán na bhFiann'.

Clare, playing against a stiff breeze, drew first blood from Sean McMahon's free. The game was man-to-man stuff, fast and tentative for the first ten minutes, the player in possession being constantly harassed and harried. Still with no real pattern emerging from the game, Tipperary led by 3 points to 1.

The breeze kept Clare mainly on the defensive with the combination of Tipperary's Declan Ryan and John Leahy posing real problems for their defence. Well into the first half Tipperary were leading by 9 points to 3 and had a strong grip on the game. I remember feeling at that time that a goal would seal it for them.

Then came one of the game's turning points. Clare stepped up a gear, and a point from Jamsie O'Connor was followed in quick succession by two great morale-boosting points from Niall Gilligan. At half-time it was Tipperary 10 points, Clare 6 points — still anybody's game.

Clare began the second half as they had finished the first with two quick points, one from Liam Doyle and the other from Conor Clancy. Then Michael Cleary tore in on the Clare goal and Brian Lohan averted what looked a certain goal. In less than 10 minutes the sides were level. The excitement was terrific. Hard, honest, committed hurling; hefty shouldering, no rancour; give and take and give more. The breeze eased slightly.

With about a quarter of an hour to go, Clare led by 17 points to 12. They now had the stronger grip on the game and were hurling superbly — speed, strength and stamina in abundance, together with lots of confidence. Ger O'Loughlin got possession on the Nally Stand side of the pitch; he was close to goal and a score looked on. A point seemed a certainty and a goal a possibility, but as the sliotar whizzed left of the upright, there were moans from the Clare supporters.

With ten minutes to go, and with Clare in the lead at 17 to 13, Liam Cahill, who came on as a sub for Tipperary, fetched on the edge of the square, turned and kicked the sliotar into the net. Tipperary were right back in the game, only a point behind in the sixty-first minute. Tension mounted, and there followed ten minutes of hectic drama and torture for the supporters of both sides. Only neutral fans could enjoy the swaying, lurching fortunes of both teams. More excitement filled the ground as Jamsie O'Connor gave Clare a two-point lead with just over five minutes to go.

However, there was more to come when, following a Tipperary 'seventy', a rebound off the Clare crossbar was whipped from mid-air by Eugene O'Neill to the net. With the clock reading 66 minutes 11 seconds, and the score at Tipperary 2:13; Clare 0:18, pandemonium broke and Tipperary followers went wild. For those at home watching the game on television, the camera showed a replay of the goal. While this was being run, midfielder Ollie Baker scored an equalising point for Clare which thousands of viewers missed because of the replay.

Clare attacked again. All eyes turned on Jamsie O'Connor who, after receiving a pass, took off at speed on the Hogan Stand side of the pitch. Striking on the run from fifty yards, he sent the sliotar sailing sweetly over the crossbar at the railway goal, putting Clare one point up.

With the clock at 68 minutes 59 seconds it was all action in this cliff-hanger climax — the game completely hanging in the balance. Suddenly, John Leahy moved inside the Clare defence and advanced menacingly between the 21- and 14-yard lines. The personification of concentration, David Fitzgerald in the Clare goal was, at this point, the last man between victory and defeat. Leahy let fly to the left of the goal. Fitzgerald, lynx-eyed, went down for the save and safely directed the ball towards the sideline. As he returned to goal he could be seen raising his eyes up to heaven. A prayer? An expression of thanks? Relief? Maybe all three.

But the drama didn't end there. This time, Tipperary, far out from the Clare goal, sent the sliotar wide in a last attempt to equalise. Finally, with the clock reading 71 minutes 6 seconds, referee Dickie Murphy of Wexford blew the final whistle, bringing down the curtain on an epic contest. What a pity there had to be a loser.

In those last ten minutes, when it seemed as if the game would slip away from Clare's grasp, they had to draw on all their inner reserves. In doing so, they displayed tremendous stoicism and stout-heartedness as well as strength and stamina — all of which were necessary to sustain their effort.

The field was full of heroes as, at different times of the game, different men rose to the demands of the moment. Ollie Baker and Colin Lynch were a great midfield partnership, while Jamsie O'Connor had a super game. He especially excelled in the second half, completely burying the nightmare of the 1995 final against Offaly when, despite his efforts, little had gone right for him. The Lohan brothers, Brian and Frank, were rock solid and gave many inspiring clearances, and Niall Gilligan and David Forde had great moments in attack.

But overall it was a team effort where every man was a link in the chain of events that brought about a famous victory.

Claremen whom I have met and profiled in my books and who always dreamed of such a day were, no doubt, there in spirit — Brendan Considine, Matt Nugent, Pa 'Fowler' McInerney, Tommy Daly and Tull Considine — *iad go léir anois imithe ar Shlí na Fírinne agus ar ndóigh ag féachaint anuas go sonasach, séanmhar, ar thoradh iontach, stairiuil — gliondar croí agus áthas an domhain ortha.*

For Clare people, the memory of this final will abide and the team will forever be part of hurling lore.

1997 All-Ireland Final
Clare Line-out

David Fitzgerald (Sixmile Bridge)

Michael O'Halloran (Sixmile Bridge), Brian Lohan (Wolfe Tones),
Frank Lohan (Wolfe Tones)

Liam Doyle (Bodyke), Sean McMahon (St Josephs/Doora-Barefield),
Anthony Daly (Clarecastle)

Ollie Baker (St Joseph's/Doora-Barefield), Colin Lynch (Lisseycasey)

James O'Connor (St Joseph's/D-B), Fergus Tuohy (Clarecastle),
P.J. O'Connell (O'Callaghan Mills)

Fergal Hegarty (Kilnamona), Conor Clancy (Kilmaley),
Ger O'Loughlin (Clarecastle)

Substitutes who also played: Niall Gilligan, Barry Murphy and David Forde.

David Fitzgerald   *James O'Connor*

On the eve of publication of this book (autumn 1999), it has just happened again! In the 1999 All-Ireland Hurling Final the score was: Cork 0:13; Kilkenny 0:12 — and note that one-point difference again.

Offaly 1998 — A Hurling Resurrection

The 1998 All-Ireland hurling final, held on Sunday, 13 September, between Offaly and Kilkenny, was a particularly stirring contest. It left spectators convinced — if convincing were needed — that the ancient game of the Celt was alive, vibrant and as exhilarating as ever.

From throw-in to final whistle, when referee Dickie Murphy of Wexford called halt to the proceedings, the fortunes of the two teams ebbed and flowed. Right up to the closing five minutes it was still anybody's game; the scoreboard read: Offaly 1:15; Kilkenny 1:13.

Throughout the contest, the outcome of the game hung in the balance. The ongoing question was which way the scales would tilt and what it would be that swung them.

Reporting on a North-Mon *v* Midleton Harty Cup match in 1991, Kevin Cashman wrote as follows:

> *On Wednesday we were given vintage Harty hurling; such hurling as has set the competition apart ever since that inspired cleric did his grand deed in 1918. Endurance, physical and moral; the will to conquer; aggression straining at, but never breaking, the boundaries into warfare: these were the prevailing values ... here, hook and block and parry and shoulder came into their own with glorious intensity.*

The same — and, indeed more — could aptly be written about the All-Ireland hurling final of 1998. There was grit and grace and grandeur and *gaisce*; there was skill and spirit and stamina; there was vim, vigour and verve; there was grim resolve, raw courage and unremitting endeavour; and there was drama and tension.

The tension took many forms. Behind me was an enthusiastic young lady supporter from Offaly. Every time D.J. Carey got possession she exclaimed, 'Oh Jesus, not D.J., not D.J.' With about a quarter of an hour to go, Kilkenny were

awarded a penalty following a foul by Martin Hanamy on
P.J. Delaney. The score stood: Offaly 1:13; Kilkenny 1:10. With
the preliminaries of placing the sliotar, gazing goalwards and
stepping clinically back completed, D.J. made ready to take the
free. In situations like this he usually shook the net. The woman
from Offaly was in acute agony — 'O Sacred Heart of Jesus,
don't let him get it, don't let him get it, that's all I'll ask You for
today!' There were sighs from the Kilkenny supporters as D.J.'s
shot whizzed over the crossbar — I felt it was a compromise
decision by the Sacred Heart.

Tom Humphries, writing in *The Irish Times* the following
Monday, successfully captured the mood of Offaly and their
supporters:

> *Ripping yarns and tall tales. This was a hurling Summer to tell the grandchildren about, won in the end by a team whose legend needs no embellishment. Offaly. It ain't what they do. It's the way they do it ... They have tattooed their personality all over this year's competition. Typically, yesterday the Faithful county's most gifted generation of hurlers played like dilettantes until they needed to roll up their sleeves and get their hands dirty. Then they dissected Kilkenny with surgical expertise ... But this victory still bore the strange character of hurling's most enigmatic team....*
>
> *In their topsy-turvy way, Offaly have resurrected themselves several times this Summer. Yesterday they did the same, recovering from a shaky start to deliver a performance that was so comprehensively vital and alive that we could only rejoice in their knack for rolling back the rock. Offaly were miserable and pallid for the first twenty minutes yesterday ....*
>
> *Well, how is this for a season; merely adequate against hapless Meath. Awful, but lucky against a weakened Wexford. Truly dire in a low intensity Leinster final against Kilkenny ... Babs Keating resigned before he was impeached. He was replaced by a big man with no reputation.*
>
> *Michael Bond. Double — oh — zero as the little joke went at the time.*
>
> *We imagined the scenes as hapless Mr Bond walked in for his first night amongst the most difficult hurlers in the country. The gentlemen of Offaly putting down their cocktails, extinguishing their cheroots, looking up and saying, 'Ah, Mr Bond, we've been expecting you.' They seemed neither stirred nor shaken by Bond's arrival ....*
>
> *They were terrible against Antrim in the All-Ireland quarter final. Expecting to be summarily guillotined by Clare, they got a draw the first day. The world assumed they would disappear after that. Indeed. Almost*

fatally bloated with over-confidence they went ten points behind the next day, but the referee blew the game up two minutes early with Offaly just in touch ... a replay was granted. Bam. Clare were sucker-punched out of the competition. Just Kilkenny left. And Offaly produced fifty minutes of perfect hurling.

In winning their fourth All-Ireland title in 18 years, Offaly carved themselves a special niche in hurling history:

- They became the very first team in the senior hurling championship to play eight games before being crowned title holders.

- They lost two games on the way: to Clare in the All-Ireland semi-final replay; and to Kilkenny in the Leinster final in a game that had a lot more good hurling and sweet striking than it was given credit for. (Offaly then re-entered the championship as defeated Leinster finalists under the current experimental system.)

- Their semi-final with Clare was unique. It was the first occasion that a semi-final went to three games and the circumstances surrounding this are dealt with in the chapter entitled 'Jimmy Cooney and Lost Time', pp. 103–106.

- They contested and won the first all-Leinster All-Ireland hurling final.

- They were the first team to become title holders through the 'back door'.

The final against Kilkenny, who had a clean sheet with victories over Dublin, Laois, Offaly and Wexford, had a number of significant moments that had a distinct bearing on the final result of 2:16 to 1:13:

- With Kilkenny in the ascendancy early in the first half, the sliotar was taken off the Offaly goal-line and cleared by Brian Whelehan.

- In the twenty-seventh minute a rasping shot by Ken O'Shea, from close range on the Hill-16 side of the pitch, was brilliantly saved and deflected onwards, and wing-wards, by Offaly goalkeeper Stephen Byrne.

- The switch of the flu-stricken Brian Whelehan, after seventeen minutes, to the forwards, from half-back was an enforced shuffle that proved to be inspirational.

- D.J. Carey failed to convert a penalty that would have levelled scores in the second half.

- Joe Erritty scored a goal, fourteen minutes into the second half, which seemed gradually to release a synergy sourced from an inner fortitude which resides in the Faithful county's psyche. This in turn produced an awesome finish of power-packed hurling.

- The gods, as is generally their wont, were present and played their part in the vagaries of the day as they frolicked with the wind in the second half.

On a day of heroic hurling, some players stood out on a slightly higher plain than others:

- When moved to the forwards, Brian Whelehan's class played an immense part in victory. He finished with a personal tally of 1:6 (three points from frees) and was made Man of the Match.

- Kevin Martin had a towering game in the half-back line and he probably won't play a better one.

- Michael Duignan, when he switched to Brian Whelehan's position at wing-back, immediately tightened the Offaly defence and gave a memorable performance.

- Johnny Pilkington did great work at midfield all through the game.

- Stephen Byrne, in goal, again confirmed that he was Offaly's find of the year.

- At full back, the phlegmatic Kevin Kinahan, mightn't have been as majestic as he was against Clare, in the 1995 final, but he didn't put a foot wrong and dealt capably with D.J. Carey when he took up residence on the edge of the square.

In all my years of watching hurling matches I have seen no team to compare with Offaly when it comes to dealing with

Kilkenny; and they do it so effectively and consistently.

In victory, Michael Bond — the Principal in Loughrea Community School and the Manager who rose from obscurity — said, 'It has made my year'.

When it was all over, he set off in glory from whence he came and, like the hero in a Western, rode into the sunset.

THE LONDON ERA

In 1900, England assumed the status of a fifth Irish province, for the purposes of GAA competitions. The championship winners in England would meet the winners of the 'home final' (that is, the championship winners in Ireland) to decide the All-Ireland title holders. The objective, no doubt, was to strengthen the promotion of Gaelic games by making provision for the many exiles working 'across the water'. By including clubs based in England in its competitions, the GAA enabled Irish people there to participate in our national pastimes. Thus, not only could Irish exiles in England play at the highest level, they could also compete against the élite exponents of the game.

In the championship of 1900, Tipperary (Two-Mile-Borris) played Galway (Ardrahan), on 21 September 1902, in the home hurling final, and had a convincing win. The final score was 6:3 to 1:5.

History was made when Tipperary (Two-Mile-Borris), captained by Ned Hayes, faced London (Desmonds), led by Cork-born Dan Horgan, in the final at Jones's Road, on 26 October 1902. A crowd of almost 10,000 spectators was treated to a fast and thrilling game.

London were in arrears at half-time, trailing by 3 points to 5 points. They added 3 points in the second half and, with less than five minutes remaining, London were leading by 6 points to Tipperary's 5. The London-Irish looked like they were about to make history, but then disaster struck — twice. A free to Tipperary saw the sliotar rushed to the net. A poor puck-out, accompanied, no doubt, by lack of concentration on the part of the London backs, led to Tipperary's scoring another goal. Then the final whistle blew and it was all over.

Here is an excerpt of an account of the game, published in the *Irish Independent GAA Golden Jubilee Number Easter 1934*:

Round the borders of the 19th and 20th centuries, Tipperary hurlers swept the field. Herculean men, fast and fearless, these Ryans and Mahers and Gleeson clans had won four out of five championships between 1896 and 1901 against the stoutest selections of Munster, Connaught, and Leinster counties. They seemed almost invincible. Led by Mike Maher, of Toberadoora, they were drawn from that superb peasantry who tilled the fertile Golden Vein country within a ten mile radius of Thurles town, where the GAA was first cradled under the patronage of Cashel's revered Prelate. Hurling tradition was in their blood. They swung ash as soon as they were able to crawl. Hurling was the sport of their youthful leisure; they hit ground balls off either hand with immense power; like war steeds they revelled in lusty combat; they played with reckless abandon — 'the honour of the village' their watchword. No fancy lifting for them. They tore their way through all opposition to victory and they had superb hurlers on their vital flanks — Tom Semple of Thurles, the peerless winger; Gleeson, Wall, and O'Keeffe of Moycarkey; Hayes and Walsh of Toberadoora. No wonder they travelled to Dublin with respectful but supreme confidence to meet those exiled hurlers who had sought a livelihood in the Saxon Capital, and still cherished their native game under difficult conditions with all the tenacity of their race.

Around about that time extensive street-paving and building contracts gave openings for men of exceptional physique in London. Friendly Irish contractors brought a few Irish hurlers across; the few brought many. All unknown to home teams, the London-Irish had gathered together and partly trained a group of super men. We had heard of Sean Oge Hanley, of Kilfinane; Dan Horgan of Ahabullogue; Coughlan, McMahon, and the McNamaras of Clare, John O'Brien of Blackrock; and Dave Roche of Limerick; but the most we could hope for was a fair and earnest game without sensing a serious challenge to Tipperary's supremacy.

The London-Irish contingent had a rocky (sea) road to Dublin. They were a weary, travel-stained, but jolly lot who disembarked on the North Wall at 2 a.m. on that bleak Sunday morning. A few faithful friends greeted them hospitably and made them comfortable at their hotel but 'twas little sleep they had, for they were already thrilled by the warmth of their home-greeting, and by the exciting prospects of the day.

Tipperary travelled by a delayed train, and amongst 10,000 eager spectators — I was a small boy then — I watched the late arrivals with something approaching hero-worship. Dressing accommodation was limited, and I recall how the teams dressed with difficulty in crowded narrow rooms crushed round with admirers.

Dublin's Lord Mayor (T. Harrington M.P.) threw the ball in at 2:10 in dull October weather; the referee was Mr John McCarthy of Kilkenny. Cheer and counter-cheer greeted the home champions and exiles alike on that memorable break away.

Tipperary swept down the field from the throw-in. Having won the toss they stormed the Railway goal. Hayes pointed, Maher had another from a free, O'Keeffe doubled in a third and despite a great defence by Flynn in the London goal, Maher tore in for Tipp's fourth point — all in the first quarter. Score, 4 to nil.

Just then London's backs opened out. Hanley, O'Brien, and Horgan surprised us with their long, accurate clearances. They stemmed the tide. Quickly the game swung to the other end. McMahon, McNamara, and Coughlan fastened on the ball, and inside five minutes rushed through three surprising points.

Then the fur flew. At every corner of the heavy pitch there were exciting duels. The visitors were standing up gallantly to the unbeaten Munster champions. Gleeson, of Tipperary, retired ill after a collision. J. Maher came on, and swiftly Semple sent his forwards away to rush Tipperary's fifth point close to the half way. Score: — Tipp. — 5 points; Exiles — 3 points.

A surprised and pleased crowd gave the London-Irish a rousing cheer as they moved off for a brief respite. They had performed handsomely. Their stout defenders held up Tipperary's storm troops. Their forwards were swift and nimble. Would they stay the hour was the question. With the wind behind them from the City in the second half, they may do better. On the other hand, Tipperary may have something in reserve. They would 'pull out' in the second half as is the champions' wont. Thus we surmised in expectancy until the ball was again swung amongst the eager groups of stern men.

And such a second half it proved! Away went the Exiles to attack, driving over in their impetuosity. Returning from every puck-out they rushed a fourth point home. When the fifth and balancing point came round the third quarter, spectators cheered wildly. Dubliners were 'with' London-Irish to a man, for the Irish-Ireland revival was then pulsating in the Capital, and London-Irish were the symbols of the scattered but yet unconquered spirit of the Irish race.

I have no record of the name (I think it was Coughlan), but when an Exile forward doubled through London's sixth point for the lead pandemonium reigned. The surrounding rails failed to hold the swaying, excited crowd. Barriers broke down with a crash, yet did good stewarding keep the pitch clear in those vivid last minutes. Sean Oge Hanley's sweeping left-handers were a feature. Then a tragic event happened. Dan Horgan, the visiting captain, playing a great game, came out to clear a loose ball. It stopped dead in a rut unexpectedly. He put his hand to it, expecting a hop, but fouled it on the sod.

Here was Tipp's last chance — one point behind and three minutes to go. Hayes took the free and dropped it on the goal mouth. In tore Mike Maher and Co. Like a whirlwind they swept the London defenders —

ball and all — through the posts for a goal! There was a wild, steely
Tipperary roar. The puck-out was weak. And in a flash Gleeson, Hayes,
and O'Keeffe were on it to goal again, just before the whistle sounded on
an epic game.

There was a wild rush of spectators; victor and vanquished were
stormed by admirers. Tipperary had held the title at home, but the
gallant losers were cheered to the echo. Their reception that day gave
them fresh heart and spirit, which was re-echoed a year later when they
achieved their ambition at the expense of Cork in another astonishing
game.

Tipperary had won their sixth All-Ireland hurling crown with
a team that included great names like Mikey Maher, Tom Semple,
Ned Hayes and Jack Gleeson. Meanwhile London, who had Sean
Oge Hanley, the outstanding hurler of that era in their ranks,
were left to ponder the might-have-beens. Sean_had won an All-
Ireland medal with his native Limerick (Kilfinane) in 1897 and, in
the mid 1950s when 'Carbery' selected 'The Best Men of My
Time' for the *Gaelic Sportsman*, he placed Sean Oge at full back.

The Tipperary footballers (Clonmel Shamrocks) made it a
great day when they defeated London (Hibernians) 3:7 to 0:2 in
the senior football final of 1900 — thus emulating their fellow
countymen who had had a similar double in 1895.

In the 1901 home final, played on 14 June 1903, Cork
(Redmonds) defeated Wexford (Blackwater) by 2:8 to 0:6. The
victory paved the way for a meeting with London (Emmets), at
Jones's Road, on 2 August 1903, and a talented Cork team
(Redmonds) were expected to win. However, they were in for a
surprise — the match finished with a final score of London 1:5;
Cork 0:4. This London team, which had created history,
consisted of all Munstermen. Interestingly, eight of them were
from Cork (it was almost an all-Cork final), four were from
Clare, three from Limerick, with Tipperary and Kerry
providing one apiece. It was a unique triumph for London — the
only occasion on which the title wasn't won by an Irish county.

Commenting on the two finals of 1900 and 1901, 'Carbery'
had this to say:

...and then we come to the epochal win of a great London Exile team of
Munster hurlers ... when London (Emmets) carried the hurling title
beyond the four seas of Éireann for the first time in history. Greater,
more thrilling still, was the contest between the London 'Desmonds' and

Tipperary. That contest was a breathless, unforgettable one, in which the exiles' ill-luck and the irrepressible finish of Tipp. gave victory to the home champions.

On 3 July 1904, in the championship hurling home final of 1902 in Tipperary, Cork (Dungourney) drew with Dublin (Faughs), the teams finishing on a score 1:7 each. Two weeks later, at the same venue, Cork left no doubt about their superiority as they took a 2:6 to 0:1 victory over Dublin.

The final was played on 11 September 1904 and Cork's opponents were London (Brian Boru). Cork (Dungourney) probably had vivid memories of the previous year — when they had suffered a surprise defeat by London — and were duly forewarned. They dominated the game from start to finish and ran up the handsome total of 3:13. London put themselves into the record book on that occasion by scoring nil; in so doing, they became the second of only two teams that failed to score in an All-Ireland hurling final — the first being Galway (1887).

Cork were captained by the great Jim Kelliher (who was later selected by 'Carbery' at centre-back when he chose his 'All-Time' fifteen in the mid 1950s). Jim had some great hurlers in his team: first cousin Tom Mahony, together with Jim Ronayne, Dan Coughlan and Tom Coughlan.

London had Paddy Mehigan in their line-out. Paddy was born on St Patrick's Day 1884 in Ardfield, County Cork, and

London-Irish Team who beat Cork, the 1901 All-Ireland Champions

was later to win fame as an outstanding sports journalist writing under the pen name 'Carbery'. He died in 1965.

The 1903 hurling championship was London's last appearance in an All-Ireland final. It was the end of an era. In the home final, played at Dungarvan on 16 July 1905, Cork (Blackrock) had had a runaway victory over Kilkenny (Threecastles) 8:9 to 0:8. On 12 November 1905, Cork faced London (Hibernians) in the final, at Jones's Road, when they secured an equally convincing win; 3:16 to London's 1:1. It was Cork's sixth All-Ireland hurling crown out of a total of seven appearances in the final. While this occasion was London's last appearance in an All-Ireland final, it also heralded the end of an era for Cork. Sixteen years would elapse before their next All-Ireland hurling success, which was not until 1919.

Willie Mackessy was on the winning Cork team of 1903. Willie was to win an All-Ireland senior football medal, with Cork in 1911, and in so doing joined the ranks of dual All-Ireland medal holders. He was the first to win medals for both hurling and football with his native county. Willie also had a keen interest in greyhounds and won the Irish Coursing Derby at Clonmel with a dog called Never Say Die.

In 1903, Limerick-born Tim Doody made his fourth successive appearance for London in an All-Ireland hurling final. Later, on the same day, at the same venue, the All-Ireland football final was played between Kerry (Tralee Mitchels) and London (Hibernians). Tim also took part in that game. It was a closer affair than the hurling final and Kerry won on the score 0:11 to 0:3. Tim, therefore, had the distinction of playing in two senior All-Ireland finals on the same day — unfortunately losing both.

London took part in five football deciders in those early years of the century. However, they were never really a match for the home champions, as the following score lines indicate.

James Nowlan, to whom Nolan Park in Kilkenny is dedicated.

1900: Tipperary (Clonmel Shamrocks) 3:7;
   London (Hibernians) 0:2
1901: Dublin (Isles of the Sea) 0:14; London (Hibernians) 0:2
1902: Dublin (Bray Emmets) 2:8; London (Hibernians) 0:4
1903: Kerry (Tralee Mitchels) 0:11; London (Hibernians) 0:3
1908: Dublin (Geraldines) 1:10; London (Hibernians) 0:4

Sam Maguire, after whom the All-Ireland senior football trophy is named, captained London in 1901 and 1903. He also played in the 1900 final.

The London era coincided with the election of that genial Kilkennyman, Alderman James Nowlan — a cooper by trade — to the office of President of the GAA.

He was unanimously elected at the Annual Convention of 1901, held in Thurles on 22 September of that year. The counties represented at the Convention were London, Dublin, Kerry, Kilkenny, Tipperary, Cork, Wexford, Limerick and Wicklow.

James Nowlan was a fluent Irish speaker and actively involved in the Gaelic League and the National Movement. 'Sliabh Ruadh' recorded that, in 1916, on 'returning from the Annual Congress held in Dublin on Easter Sunday, Alderman James Nowlan, President of the GAA, was arrested in John Street, Kilkenny, on Tuesday evening and conveyed to Kilkenny Prison under a strong military escort'.

He was the Association's seventh President and the first Kilkennyman to occupy the position.

He had the unique distinction of remaining in the job for a period of twenty years — by far the longest period ever for any one individual to hold this office.

James Nowlan left Kilkenny to take up residence in Dublin in 1920. When he resigned as President in 1921, he was made a life member of the Central Council in appreciation of his contribution and dedication to Gaelic Games over two decades. The Kilkenny county ground, Nowlan Park, was dedicated to James Nowlan in 1928 and commemorates his memory and his enormous contribution to the GAA.

He died on 30 June 1924.

General Secretaries/Directors General

Luke O'Toole

The position of GAA Secretary, as we know it today, could really be said to have come into existence with the election of Luke O'Toole at the Central Council meeting of 6 January 1901, which was held at Thurles. He defeated Michael Cusack by 19 votes to 17. A former Secretary, R.T. (Dick) Blake of Meath, was proposed but ruled out because he was not a member of an affiliated club.

The list hereunder shows those who had previously held the post, and the year their election:

- 1884 Michael Cusack (Clare)
- 1885 (Honorary Secretaries) Michael Cusack (Clare), John McKay (Cork), John Wyse Power (Kildare)
- 1886 Timothy O'Riordan (Cork), John Wyse Power (Kildare), John Boyle O'Reilly (Dublin)
- 1887 Timothy O'Riordan (Cork), John Boyle O'Reilly (Dublin) and James Moore (Dundalk)
- 1888 William Prendergast (Clonmel)
- 1889 P.B. Clery (Caherconlish, County Limerick)
- 1890 Maurice Moynihan (Tralee)
- 1891 Patrick Tobin (Dublin)
- 1892 Patrick Tobin (Dublin)
- 1893 Patrick Tobin (Dublin)
- 1894 David Walsh (Cork)
- 1895 R.T. Blake (Ladyrath, Navan, County Meath)
- 1896 R.T. Blake
- 1897 R.T. Blake
- 1898 Frank B. Dinneen (Limerick) — a former President of the GAA
- 1899 Frank B. Dinneen
- 1900 Frank B. Dinneen

Luke O'Toole, a native of Wicklow, took office at a time when the GAA was still struggling and very much in its infancy. During this period it was a scattered and disjointed organisation, badly in need of co-ordination.

His main task was to focus on its chief objectives, establish unity of purpose, create structures and generate funds. The remuneration package given to Luke consisted of travelling expenses and 15 per cent of gross gate receipts.

The challenge facing Luke O'Toole was immense and in many ways awesome, but he was successful in tackling the task. Under his stewardship, the establishment of the Provincial Councils was completed, and this greatly facilitated the running of the All-Ireland championships. The Munster and Leinster Councils were put in place in 1900.

The Munster Council was established following a meeting in Tipperary on 14 October, at which Patrick McGrath, (Tipperary) and P.J. Hayes (Limerick) were elected President and Secretary respectively. On 4 November, the Leinster Council was created following a meeting at which Alderman James Nowlan (Kilkenny) was elected President, and Watt Hanrahan (Wexford) was voted in as Secretary.

The Connaught council was formed following a meeting at Ryan's Hotel, Claremorris, on 9 November 1902. The meeting was attended by delegates from Mayo, Galway and Roscommon, and Joe McBride (Mayo) was elected Chairman. Michael C. Shine (Galway) was made Treasurer and Frank Dorr (Roscommon) became the Council's Secretary.

Ulster delegates met at Armagh on 22 March 1903 for the purpose of forming a council for their province. Their elections yielded the following results: President — George Martin (Antrim); Vice-President — M.V. Nolan (Tyrone); Secretary — L.F. O'Kane (Derry); Trustees — Messrs Power (Antrim) and O'Reilly (Cavan).

Following a Central Council meeting on 3 January 1904, it was decided to procure offices at 68 Upper O'Connell Street, Dublin. Prior to that, Central Council meetings, held in Dublin, took place at Luke O'Toole's residence at 29 Mount Pleasant Square, during his time in office. Croke Park was acquired and developed in 1913.

Luke O'Toole (centre) with Michael Collins (left) and Harry Boland (right)

Luke O'Toole was at the helm during the turbulent political days of the War of Independence and the ensuing Civil War. In the early days of August 1918 he advised all county boards to follow the Central Council directive to play Gaelic games, without permit, on Sunday 4 August, in defiance of the orders of the police authorities.

The Tailteann games were revived in 1924, if only for a short duration.

Luke served under five Presidents of the GAA:

- James Nowlan (Kilkenny), elected in 1901
- Dan McCarthy (Dublin), elected in 1921
- Patrick D. Breen (Wexford), elected in 1924
- William P. Clifford (Limerick), elected in 1926
- Sean Ryan (Dublin), elected in 1928.

Luke's interest in GAA affairs took root early in his life. In his time he refereed many matches, including the 1902 All-Ireland senior hurling final in which Cork had a runaway 3:13 to no score victory over London. He made a wonderful contribution to the GAA in its infant years and was still in office when he died in July 1929.

Padraig O'Caoimh

On Saturday, 3 September 1929, Padraig O'Caoimh was elected General Secretary of the GAA at a meeting of the Central Council. At that time he was known to thousands of GAA followers as Paddy O'Keeffe. In a very close contest he defeated Frank Burke, dual All-Ireland medalist for Dublin, by 11 votes to 10.

Paddy was an active volunteer during the War of Independence before his capture and imprisonment. On his release he became Secretary of Cork County Board, which was the biggest Administration unit in the GAA at the time. He was only 21 years of age.

He was perceived by most people as a Corkman, but he was actually born in Roscommon, a fact that wasn't widely known. He was often affectionately referred to as 'Paddy-O' and his memory is perpetuated in the re-naming of the Cork Athletic Grounds as Pairc Uí Chaoimh.

He was an excellent referee and demonstrated this to the full in his firm handling of some tempestuous contests between Limerick and Tipperary in the 1920s. He was also an enthusiastic supporter of the Irish language and was intensely patriotic.

The Railway Cup competition and the minor championships were his brain child and it was he who initiated the practice of having the ownership of GAA grounds vested in trustees. This strategy ensured both control and continuity of these properties for the sport itself. Paddy also pioneered the promotion of Gaelic games in our schools and colleges.

The key hall-marks that enabled him to steer the Association from strength to strength over 35 years were his leadership qualities, attention to detail, exceptional organisational ability and total dedication to the task in hand. All of these attributes were allied to his high levels of energy and his keen intellect.

Marcus de Búrca in an article published in the GAA Centenary Supplement of *The Irish Times* had this to say of 'Paddy O':

> *The secret of O'Keeffe's success, the key to his outstanding work for the GAA over such a long period, some 45 years, if one includes his years as Cork County Secretary, lay in the rare combination of idealist and*

realist in one personality. No other major figure in the GAA before or since had this dual ability; none knew with such unerring intuition when to be one or the other. Added to this were a charming, outgoing cheerful disposition which won him countless friends and admirers even outside the Association, and administrative ability of a high order, which he maintained even in his later years despite recurring bouts of ill-health that he concealed from all but his closest friends.

Paddy served under twelve Presidents of the Association, the last of whom was Alf Murray of Armagh, who had this to say following Paddy's death in May 1964:

He gave the Association a place in the life of the country, no other body could aspire to. He engendered an amazing goodwill which is our most important asset. His attitude was the criterion of all our efforts. He was our most competent visionary, our most efficient businessman.

Padraig O'Caoimh

Seán Ó Síocháin

Following the death of Padraig O'Caoimh, in 1964, Seán Ó Síocháin took over the position and he was ideally equipped for the task in hand.

In his younger years he excelled at hurling and played football in all grades for his native Cork. During his teaching days in Dublin he played with Clan na Gael and was honoured with the captaincy of the County team.

He was appointed Assistant to Padraig O'Caoimh in 1946, which, as he used to say himself, increased the Headquarters staff by 50 per cent to a total of three people. As a result, for eighteen years, he was in close touch with the developments and progress that took place within the GAA. In that time he demonstrated a range of qualities that made him a great Ambassador for the Association both at home and abroad.

No question ever fazed him, as shown when he was asked at a large social gathering — in the US, I think — which was the better player, Paddy Kennedy or Mick O'Connell. Drawing on his diplomacy to the full, he said that for consistency Paddy Kennedy had no equal. He then gave the accolade for style to Mick O'Connell.

Seán also became known for the quality of his voice. Writing in *The Irish Times* GAA Centenary supplement he recollected:

> *My first official link with Croke Park was to be invited by my predecessor, Padraig O'Caoimh, to bring a group of fellow-students from St Patrick's Teachers' Training College in Drumcondra to sing the National Anthem in Irish over the air at the All Ireland Football Final in 1933.*
>
> *On that occasion, we stood outside the open door of the Radio Éireann box, which was in a raised position between the Old Hogan Stand and the then Long Stand. On subsequent occasions we stood on the steps of the Hogan nearest to the box with our own microphone on an extended lead.*

His fine singing voice was subsequently heard through three popular radio programmes — 'Ireland is Singing' in the late 1930s, 'Round the Fire' through much of the 1940s and in the late 1950s 'Balladmakers Saturday Night'. He sang at home and overseas and did four concert tours of the United States of America.

Seán's outgoing and gregarious personality was matched by a great speaking voice. His presence always radiated that great indefinable trait, charisma.

In office he continued the great work of Padraig O'Caoimh and he was one of those fortunate people whose job was also a labour of love. He was always very aware and appreciative of the incalculable contribution made to the GAA by its vast number of volunteer workers.

In 1979, he resigned from the post of Director General. From then until 1982 he was Ceann Áras Director and as such was involved in a fund-raising campaign that brought in over £1,000,000 for the new Headquarters.

Seán was born in 1914 in Cill na Martra, near Macroom, County Cork, and grew up in a rural atmosphere that was steeped in Gaelic traditions. When he died in February 1997,

Gaeldom mourned a son whose name will forever be synonymous with GAA affairs.

Seán Ó Síocháin

Liam Mulvihill

With the resignation of Seán Ó Síocháin in 1979, the reins of office were taken over by Liam Mulvihill, a former National School teacher and Schools Inspector. Interestingly, he was born in 1946, the year Seán Ó Síocháin first took up duty at Croke Park as Assistant to Padraig O'Caoimh.

Liam came of farming stock and grew up in south County Longford on a large farm, which straddled three parishes. All the family were interested in GAA affairs. It was in the blood. On his mother's side, the Donlons, both male and female, were very involved, and an uncle held office for over thirty years on the Longford County Board.

Liam's native parish was Kenagh, but he received his primary education at Ballymahon National School, which was closer to home. In third class he had the good luck to have as his teacher Tom Casey — a man who had a deep interest in education and sport. Tom introduced Liam and his classmates to hurling and football. He had an All-Ireland colleges senior football medal from 1948 when he had captained St Mel's to their first All-Ireland title. He used to take out the medal and show it to them, and tell them that they would 'never equal that'.

Tom was a great educator and sports mentor but he was a poor prophet. Four of his pupils later won All-Ireland Colleges medals with St Mel's.

Liam captained the primary school team for three years but they were knocked out each year by a neighbouring parish. It was a disappointment for Liam because prior to his becoming captain the school had won three in a row. In those early years of childhood he learned to accept defeat with equanimity. According to his philosophy:

> *Sometimes you can be lucky to play with unsuccessful teams. You learn that success is not everything. It also gives you a greater appreciation of small successes. Of course you would always want to win but it's important to be able to take defeat. I have heard people ask how do players go out year after year and play for Longford and not taste success. You see, it's about the pride that goes with playing the game and the honour of wearing the jersey.*

On one occasion, Liam played with Ballymahon under-14 team only to be quickly reminded that Kenagh was his native parish. Back he came, learning at an early age how jealously a parish guards and cherishes its native talent.

Kenagh, a small parish, gradually built successful teams 'from a good grouping of young chaps'. In time they went on to win county titles at under-21, junior and intermediate level. Liam received his secondary education at that great football nursery, St Mel's — a college that dominated football in Leinster for long periods. Between 1933 and 1948 they captured fourteen Leinster crowns, losing out only in 1939 and 1944 to St Finian's of Mullingar. After a lean spell in the 1950s — their only success was in 1951 — they came back with a bang to win four in a row in Leinster from 1961 to 1964 inclusive.

Liam recalls winning 'two or three Leinster junior titles, three Leinster senior medals and one All-Ireland medal' while at St Mel's. He played in the right half-back position on the all-conquering 1963 team. It was a hard campaign. Having won in Leinster, they defeated St Colman's (Newry) at Kells by 1:10 to 2:5 in the semi-final. In the final they had the honour of playing in Croke Park and crowned a great campaign with a 1:6 to 2:2 victory over St Brendan's (Killarney).

The following year they again reached the final after disposing of Newry CBS 3:10 to 3:2 at the semi-final stage. Their opponents were old rivals, St Jarlath's. Liam was a 'natural half-back', but a series of injuries had left him operating at corner forward. He recalls scoring the equalising point in the final at Athlone. However, the team's luck ran out in the replay at Tullamore when St Jarlath's had an impressive win, 1:10 to 0:4.

Liam's performances at club and college level brought him to the notice of the Longford selectors and he proceeded to represent the county in all grades. While studying at St Patrick's Training College, Drumcondra, he became a Longford selector. That finished his days at county level because a rule in Longford prohibited selectors from also being players.

However, his brother Tom kept the family flag flying at county senior level. He was a sub on the 1966 team that beat Galway in the home final of the League, and he played against New York in the two-leg final at Longford and Croke Park. It was won by Longford on the aggregate score of 1:18 to 0:17. Two years later Tom Mulvihill was part of the Longford team that won the Leinster title. Playing a lovely brand of football, Longford went within an ace of defeating Kerry in the All-Ireland semi-final — losing by only two points, 2:13 to 2:11. A remarkable feature of the Longford performance was that they conceded only four frees in the entire hour.

Liam gradually became more deeply immersed in the administrative side of GAA affairs. In 1969, at the age of twenty-three, he was Vice-Chairman of the Longford County Board, and a year later he was elected Chairman. He had to relinquish the post in 1971 when he was chosen as the Longford delegate to the Central Council. It is interesting to note that since 1971 Liam has had an unbroken link with the Central Council — initially as Longford delegate until 1979, and thereafter in the capacity of Director General.

In tandem with his GAA activities, Liam was also pursuing his academic studies. Having qualified as a National School teacher, he did his H.Dip. in Education, together with an Arts degree. That was followed by a Masters in Education and his appointment to the post of schools inspector. In the very early days of his inspectorate apprenticeship he 'learned from a very wise senior colleague the importance in any human assessment of always highlighting the strengths and positive aspects as well as the weaknesses and shortcomings'.

When the position of Director General became vacant in 1979, Liam 'felt very fulfilled' both as a Schools Inspector and, in the GAA world, as the Longford delegate to the Central Council. He didn't give a thought to applying for the position of Director General, but a Longford colleague had other ideas. He obtained an application form from Central Council and approached Liam, saying, 'Wouldn't it be nice to have a Longford man in there with a shout?' Liam duly submitted the form and went through the subsequent formalities.

Some time later he was in Croke Park, 'standing around with others and chatting', awaiting a Central Council meeting, which would follow another meeting being chaired by President Con Murphy. An official came out from the other meeting, took Liam by the arm and led him to one side. 'They'd like a word with you inside,' he said. Liam assumed that it was something they wanted to enquire about. Instead, Con Murphy told him that he was being offered the job of Director General, and asked would he accept it.

Liam, somewhat nonplussed and conscious of the need to inform his employer, asked how long he had to decide. 'Ten to fifteen minutes,' was the reply. Liam Mulvihill's appointment to the post of Director General of the GAA was officially announced at Congress, which took place shortly afterwards.

By the time of the announcement, Liam was back playing junior football with Kenagh, and there was great media attention when the new Director General lined out. Liam continued playing up to 1984.

One of his ambitions as Director General was 'to modernise the organisation, enhance its image, effectively sell our games and ensure that it received the credit it deserved'. Matters like amateur status, playing rules and discipline also formed part of his agenda.

In more recent times he has given much thought to competition structures:

I saw hurling in particular as requiring examination. I didn't want a situation where the few dominated the many. I was acutely aware that success spread around — the variety and glamour that new faces bring — is the very life blood of the association and the oxygen on which it thrives.

Liam's aim was to create a system where, at club and county level, 'players would get a reasonable programme of games. The model that would emerge would be streamlined and enhanced as time progressed.' He is pleased with the present senior hurling structure which, he realises, 'will be the subject of ongoing scrutiny', and he instances the 'improved standard of our games'. He feels that the football model at present being looked at could very well be replicated in the hurling structure.

Without doubt, the greatest single undertaking during Liam's stewardship has been the redevelopment of Croke Park — heading at the turn of the century towards the halfway completion stage. He admits that the programme was 'incredibly ambitious' but believes that it will have 'far greater significance for the Association than might have been initially realised'.

The completion of the finished product will coincide, more or less, with the hundredth Anniversary of Luke O'Toole's election in January 1901. What a changed scene — a scene of progress and confidence; a scene that would surely fill Luke and his contemporaries with pride and joy.

To Liam Mulvihill falls the task and the honour of leading and guiding the GAA into the challenging years of the next century and the new millennium.

The GAA is in safe and good hands.

Liam Mulvihill
Courtesy of the GAA

Also by Brendan Fullam

Giants of the Ash

'A great hurling book ... *Giants of the Ash* has the nation's history woven into it.... Conversation courses through the pages as it flows through the living body of the game.' *Irish Times*

'A winner ... the work of a warm appreciator and a modest recorder, who has done a fine service to the literature of hurling.' *Tipperary Star*

A magnificent record of the game of hurling, through the thoughts and memories of the people who played it at the highest level through the century — Willie John Daly, Christy Ring, Mick Mackey, John Doyle and all the big names.

ISBN 0-86327-346-7

Hurling Giants

Another classic from the author of the greatest hurling book of all time. Interviews, photographs, team choices, autographs and players' text all capture the views, memories, nostalgia, fulfilment and friendships associated with a truly unique sport — the game of hurling.

ISBN 0-86327-666-0

Also by Brendan Fullam

Legends of the Ash

Author Brendan Fullam has researched, interviewed and written about hurling legends from all over the country for eighteen years. In *Legends of the Ash*, he brings to a culmination his unique record of the game of hurling, begun with *Giants of the Ash* and continued with *Hurling Giants*.

Legends of the Ash, the third and final classic book in the series, is packed with interviews, photographs, team choices, autographs and the players' own writing. Nine of the players are still playing, some are recently retired from the game, and many are simply legendary heroes. The book captures the memories, nostalgia, fulfilment, skill, great games and friendship associated with a truly unique sport — the game of hurling.

Illustrated in colour and black & white, *Legends of the Ash* is a tribute to a great game, a treasure for all sports enthusiasts, and a great read.

- Includes sixty-eight players and the legendary voices of Mícheál O'Hehir and Mícheál Ó Muircheartaigh
- Covers the entire timespan of the GAA
- Features six camogie players

ISBN 0-86327-667-9

Available from:
WOLFHOUND PRESS
68 Mountjoy Square
Dublin 1
Tel: +353 1 874 0354
Fax: +353 1 872 0207